Those who serve the Church dedicate th[...]
teaching the grace of God in Christ Jesus[...]
his servants to lose their lives, take up th[...]
following and discipleship are grounded [...]
his Son, Jesus Christ. Sadly, due to the weakness of the flesh, the assaults of the devil, and the great stresses of this world, servants of the Church fail to hold in their own lives the very Good News they profess in their calling—to the detriment of their own bodies and souls. Dr. Eckrich has dedicated himself to care for those who care for God's people and to direct them to the grace of God that is sufficient for all their needs. *Vocation and Wellness* is a gift to the Church and her servants as the author diagnoses with his physician's skill the symptoms and root causes of the church worker's physical and spiritual disease. He directs them and all God's people to the medicine, cure, and true healer: Jesus Christ who makes all things well. This book should not only be read but also be put into practice by those who serve the Church. This can be done as laity read it and lovingly encourage the servants of their congregation toward wellness and health in body and soul. All should follow the good doctor's prescription and find energy, wellness, and joy for service in the grace of God in Christ Jesus.

Rev. Bart Day
Executive Director, Office of National Mission
Lutheran Church Missouri Synod (LCMS)
Ordained LCMS Clergy

We are each born with a unique set of genes that will influence our health and affect the way we think and act as well as our susceptibility to disease. However, there is ample evidence that our attitudes, lifestyle, habits, and diet can affect these genetic foundations and greatly impact how we experience the world, value both ourselves and our relationships, and avoid disease. In Dr. Eckrich's book on wellness, he uses his training in both theology and medicine to provide an insightful and pragmatic lesson plan for a life well lived. As a physician and scientist, I was most drawn to his comments on diet, exercise, rest, and relaxation. While not overwhelming the non-scientist reader with technical details, the medical reasons for what he advocates are strongly based on current knowledge. The material is presented in a well-written, reader friendly format; questions are clearly posed, ample backgrounds are provided, and well-reasoned and practical suggestions are given. This textbook provides unique and thoughtful perspectives and valuable suggestions on how to pursue a healthful life that should be of broad interest to all readers.

Fred Gorelick, M.D.
Professor of Medicine and Cell Biology
Deputy Director, Yale MD-PhD Program
Yale University School of Medicine

Dr. Eckrich writes a compelling book encouraging us that coming to terms with God's generosity of grace in Jesus is one of the key things we need to do in order to live a balanced and healthy life—not just spiritually, but physically, emotionally, vocationally and financially. We have found this particularly true as we help people be wise with money and live generously.

Brad Hewitt
CEO Thrivent Financial

This book is as remarkable as it is accessible. Eckrich offers a scripturally sound, classically orthodox, and terrifically relevant vision for living a healthy, holy, happy life in Christ in the midst of the challenges facing Christians today. Given his long experience in caring for Christian ministers of every stripe, coupled with his own deep and authentic faith in Christ, Eckrich offers a kind of "middle way" between uncritical appropriation of every new diet and exercise fad and a kind of paranoid Puritanism which would have devout Christians simply try and pray away their problems. Ultimately Dr. Eckrich's program works because it founds wellness in the foundation of all things—life in Christ Jesus—and so recasts wellness and self-care, not as self-indulgence but as worship, an act of gratitude and praise to the God Who has chosen to make us His temples.

Fr. Dominic McManus, OP
Dominican Friar, Province of Albert the Great
Chicago, IL

Nice work in integrating church professional self-care with the Christian Gospel. Having clergy who are physically, emotionally, and spiritually healthy and committed disciples of Christ is not an oxymoron. Thank you for dispelling the notion that to be a servant of Christ means sacrificing ourselves, physically and emotionally, to the Lord.

Rev. Roy Oswald
Executive Director, Center for EQ-HR Skills (www.eqhrcenter.org)
Former Senior Consultant for Alban Institute
Ordained ELCA Pastor

For those who tend to think "too much is never enough" in pouring themselves into people and projects, there's healing in this great read. Hear today, be well tomorrow ... or at least be on the way to the wellness God intends, offers, and promises. It's right here through tried and true wisdom earned by decades of experience with thousands of patients. Want to do something immeasurably good for those you serve? Read this book! And for goodness' sake, read it for yourself!

Phyllis Wallace
Host, *Woman to Woman* Talk Radio
Family Counselor and Author

Dr. John's passion for church workers is unmistakable in this refreshing book. His unique perspective as a physician is coupled with a deep faith and understanding of how God works in the practical, daily lives of his people. This book gives hope for renewal of energy that is critical to prevent burnout and to restore vocational wellness. The flow of the book itself gives testimony to the flow of energy and love from one's relationship with God ("we") that pushes aside anxiety, personal struggles of worth, and all the other issues that come from trying to prove self ("me"). At every turn, there are practical suggestions and exercises to help make wellness part of the church worker's lifestyle. This book will be a blessing to so many!

Dr. David J. Ludwig
Professor of Clinical Psychology, Lenoir Rhyne University
Hickory, NC

In a world that encourages a focus on personal health and wellness as an end in itself, Dr. Eckrich reminds us that we are called to something more. He not only illustrates how a focus on wellness connects to our vocations but also demonstrates how God—through his unfailing grace—equips and empowers each of us on this journey. With our Wellness Backpack stocked with God's good gifts, we will be spiritually and physically energized to live out our respective vocations!

James F. Sanft
President and CEO, Concordia Plan Services
LCMS Health and Benefits Services

In the midst of a wealth of practical advice for living well, Dr. Eckrich never strays far from the idea of an eternal perspective that ultimately enables us to renew ourselves and live the lives that we desire and that God intends. Theological points of difference among faiths aside, Dr. Eckrich clearly establishes our saving relationship with Jesus Christ, the Creator of the Universe, as the key to our wellness journey. He shows how through that relationship, the work of the Holy Spirit, and God's grace we are able to put on a healthy and new self in every area of life. Important to this process is taking our focus off ("me") and placing it on ("we")—that is, our relationship with our Lord. *Vocation and Wellness* is a wonderful resource and is both pragmatic and spiritual.

Ty Dodge
Chairman Emeritus, Realty South
Elder, Briarwood Presbyterian Church (PCA)
Lay counselor, Bible teacher

We rely on our physicians and other healthcare professionals to look after our wellbeing. We trust them to give us good guidance and counsel to help cure what ails us or to avoid problems before they arise. The best medical professionals recognize that humans are complex beings and that our health is not limited to physical fitness. Over the course of his distinguished career Dr. John Eckrich has demonstrated extraordinary interest, not only in the health of patients under his charge, but also in the Lord's servants. A range of physical, mental, emotional, spiritual, and other health challenges face people whose dedication to serving others does not always include sufficient attention to their own needs. Dr. Eckrich's observation of the particular concerns of church workers was inspiration for the founding of Grace Place Wellness. This succinct and insightful book is drawn from years of experience helping others to live healthy lives. In it, we benefit from valuable insights and useful, practical applications designed to help us grow in our reliance on the grace of God in Christ Jesus and to embrace the importance of balanced self-care. Here we have a prescription from a medical doctor who genuinely cares about the health of our bodies, our minds, and our souls.

Rev. Dr. Patrick Ferry, M.Div, Ph.D.
President, Concordia University
Mequon, WI
Vice President, Concordia University System
Ordained LCMS Pastor

I take this book personally and hope you will too. It's a strange blessing to hit the stone wall of our limitations, but it's then that God reminds us we're still and wholly his beloved children. I'm putting *Vocation and Wellness* on a shelf with my devotion books because wellness is integral to godliness.

Rev. Dr. Dale Meyer
President, Concordia Seminary
St. Louis, MO

John Eckrich's book is a little gem. It's an everything-you-always-wanted-to-know compendium of the best advice and information to keep your body going strong and your service to God and others joyful. A great companion to one of Grace Place's wonderful retreats for church workers, this book will serve as a great review of all you've learned and a good reminder to keep doing what you know you should do! Loaded with common sense, good advice, and full of the grace that nourishes your soul, this book will help you stay joyful in service, balanced in your lifestyle choices and daily renewed in the refreshing grace of God.

Ruth N. Koch, M.A., NCC
Mental Health Educator
Co-author of *Speaking the Truth In Love: How to Be an Assertive Christian*

Vocation AND Wellness

RENEW YOUR ENERGY FOR CHRISTIAN LIVING

JOHN D. ECKRICH, M.D.

TENTH
POWER

Elgin, IL · Tyler, TX

TENTHPOWERPUBLISHING
www.tenthpowerpublishing.com

Design by Inkwell Creative

Softcover ISBN 978-1-938840-09-8

e-book ISBN 978-1-938840-10-4

10 9 8 7 6 5 4 3 2 1

To all those Called and called to serve
Christ and share the good news of the
Gospel through their vocations.

TABLE OF CONTENTS

FOREWORD 13

ACKNOWLEDGEMENTS 15

INTRODUCTION 17

1. RENEWABLE ENERGY WELLNESS 23

2. FINDING WELLNESS IN THE SCRIPTURES 29

3. BALANCING WELLNESS OF BODY, MIND, AND SOUL 45

4. THE BALANCED WELLNESS BACKPACK 53

APPENDIX 91

    Burnout Inventory 93

    Wellness Support Team Guidelines 99

    Retreats and Other Resources for Wellness of Mind 105

    Chanting Guidelines 107

    Family Devotional Resources 109

    Fasting Guidelines 111

    Stretching and Meditation Workout Routine 115

    Painter/Pointer Communication Typography Scale 121

    Bible Study Guide for Small Groups 123

TABLE OF CONTENTS

FOREWORD

In this increasingly secular "post-Christian" world most are challenged by difficulties of American 'performance lives' with rest, relaxation, and wholeness. Jesus' mandates for refreshing ourselves with attention to body, mind, and soul are all too often and too easily overlooked. *Vocation and Wellness: Renew Your Energy for Christian Living* is a practical guide through the vicissitudes of our busy lives calling us back to our foundations of life, health, and spirituality. Dr. John Eckrich has a long history of guiding individuals through this process, time-tested in Grace Place Wellness Ministries, which he founded and which have served people well for more than 17 years. The wisdom of this mature medical practitioner, who is also a committed and fervent Christian, calls us to live centered, balanced lives. His practical suggestions, and in particular his Wellness Backpack, are important and easily understandable guides for all. This self-help compendium will be a tonic to all who read it.

John W. Kilgore, M.D.

Board Certified Internist and Cardiologist
Reverend Canon, Christ Church Cathedral, Episcopal Diocese of Missouri

ACKNOWLEDGEMENTS

Grace Place Wellness Ministry is such a collaborative effort. All along the way on this, my wellness walk, I have been mentored and accompanied by so many fellow disciples, many with years of experience in congregational ministry or parochial education. I wish to personally thank Rev. Dr. David Ludwig and his wife, Kathy, from Hickory, N.C., the author of many of the relational, emotional, and intellectual guidelines of our program derived from his years of counseling and professorship. In the early days, our pastoral retreat leaders were Rev. Dar and Jan Karsten (pastor and nurse, respectively), who focused on challenges of life in the parish. In the midlife of Grace Place Wellness, Rev. Dr. Bill Yancey and his wife, Dr. Valerie Yancey, R.N., brought insight into the loss and grief that can rob energy from the living, both from a personal viewpoint and ministry path.

Additionally, Revs. Drs. David Smith, Bryan Salminen, and Lee Hovel provided invaluable leadership in counseling and parish ministry leadership. Ministers of Music David Christian and Barry Bobb have added remarkable perspectives into the unique challenges of music ministry service, and their wives, Dr. Judy Christian and Donna Bobb (both parochial educators), have guided us in regard to the stresses of the teaching ministry. Further, Eustolio Gomez, Director of Financial Education from Concordia Plan Services of the LCMS, has brought fiscal wisdom and understanding to virtually all of our attendees over the past 17 years.

More recently, the program leadership of Grace Place Wellness has been assumed by Rev. Dr. Darrell Zimmerman. Darrell and his wife, Carol, (an RN) attended the first Grace Place Wellness Retreat in 1999. Darrell has innovatively and energetically become our Vice President and Director of Programming and leads our retreats.

I also wish to recognize and thank Melissa Hower, the Grace Place Wellness Mission Advancement Officer, and Beth McAnallen for their invaluable secretarial and administrative assistance.

In the last year and a half, God has graciously gifted Grace Place Wellness with a new CEO and President, Randy Fauser, who brings enormous passion and knowledge to the funding and management of our organizational mission. Grace Place Wellness must generate substantial funding to continue to *gift* our ministry to professional church workers. Randy is the right man at the right time. All of this has been wisely guided by an extraordinary board of directors and our leadership, including John Obermann, Jim Dankenbring, Mark Kuhlmann, Jeff Hollingsworth, and Bill Mattson, who originally challenged me to prepare this text. Grace Place Wellness is also blessed by generous donors.

Furthermore, I want to recognize the invaluable help of Mark Zimmermann in editing this text and beautifully refining devotional material. Additionally, I want to thank fellow physician and Episcopal priest Rev. Dr. John Kilgore, for his encouragement and review.

At the last, I want to thank my dear wife of 40 years, Kathy, also a registered nurse, volunteer, and mother. Her support, as well as that of my children, Christopher, Molly, and Michael, has been irreplaceable. Thanks to all and praise God for his goodness and grace.

INTRODUCTION

"Dr. Eckrich, can you see one more patient this afternoon?" asks my nurse. "Sure, send them in," I respond with a quick glance at the pile of charts in front of me. "It's the new pastor from St. Stephen's congregation," she chimes in. "Looks like he needs a friend."

He did. What greeted me was a somber, weary, rotund fellow who looked as if he was carrying the full weight of his faith community on his back. His shoulders were hunched forward, his eyes were reddened, and his responses slow and deliberate.

"I understand you're the new padre at St. Stephen's. What brings you in today?" I queried. "Headaches," he answered. "Constant headaches like a vise around my head." Trying to lighten the conversation a bit, I chirped, "Maybe that clerical collar is a little too tight." He took a moment to digest my attempt at humor, then soulfully responded, "I think you're probably right on target."

Here's the real story. Pastor had just taken a call at St. Stephen's six months ago and was settling into his new role of shepherding, uprooting and resettling his wife and children, and getting used to urban ministry. He had moved from a small rural congregation in the upper Midwest.

St. Stephen's had a parsonage or *manse*, as had his previous parish. This aging structure had sat empty for a few years and was clearly in need of a few updates. In fact, he shared that his dear wife had already begun to enhance their new home by surprising him with some simple and lively wallpaper and a dash of paint here and there in the family room and kitchen.

However, as a welcoming gesture, several women of the congregation, whose husbands served on the church council, had surprised his wife by bringing over coffee cake and rolls to welcome her to St. Stephen's.

A week after the ladies' visit, the pastor was called into a *special* elders' meeting. He was strictly informed that the parsonage was solely the property of the parish, and that any changes to its character had to be reviewed and approved by the board. The elders suggested that pastor have a "heart-to-heart" with his wife and immediately chastise her for "coloring outside the guidelines."

His headaches began that very evening and have persisted for months ever since, interrupting his wake and sleep, as he struggles with so much *hurt* within his family life. It is to the point where his wife can barely bring herself to worship in the same congregation. The distress at home is affecting the joy and vibrancy of pastor's ministry service; his energy is sapped. The turbulence of this turmoil is producing real physical signs and symptoms—high blood pressure, rapid weight gain, and bodily fatigue. He is not well.

There is a cascade of interrelated dysfunctions occurring in this church servant's life, leading to spiraling unhealthy wellness choices and behaviors. The turbulence in ministry is burning up his health so quickly that he even finds himself at a loss for a storehouse of resilient energy.

My guess is that, no matter what your vocation, you have been in one of these anxiety-producing, energy-consuming life situations resulting from career challenges, family conflicts, financial tensions, or perhaps even struggles in your faith life. Faced with these issues, you've had to make wellness choices in your practical daily walk with Jesus. Might it be helpful for us to "pause" and examine where we are along our respective health journeys?

There are many health and wellness books out there, but this one is different. It is from the perspective of a Christian doctor who treats many who are involved in church work. I would like to apply what I have learned from my care of these patients to all people seeking energizing health and wellness in body, mind, and soul in their Christian lives and service.

As a Christian primary care physician, I am happy to walk with you on your pursuit of energy for living and serving. As we start our journey together, let me share my story with you. The patients under my medical care fill virtually every category of church work, in addition to people of all walks of life. I have spent the last 42 years taking care of the health and wellness of pastors, teachers, and laity of all vocations through my service as a board-certified internist and gastroenterologist.

Again and again in my practice I observed frequent physical consequences of stress—heart disease, obesity, poor eating and exercise patterns, hypertension, and immune-modulated illnesses. Certainly there were emotional and relational sequelae of stress and anxiety, with marital strife, child-rearing dysfunction, and a slew of workplace aggravations.

There were clear-cut financial pressures due to salary and compensation challenges, educational debt, and adjustments to living with limited means. And, I truly believe within the more transparent and trusting moments of our doctor-patient-friend office meetings, there were spiritual doubts and hurts expressed or implied. All of these factors robbed life and service of energy, of vitality, and joy.

What I observed as common denominators in these many variations of distress, disorder, and disease were a lack of reliance on God's grace (how we relate to God) and a lack of balanced self-care (how we relate to ourselves and others). Both depleted energy from living and serving.

I've learned these lessons from myself and my patients, and especially from those in the vocation of professional church service. Church workers are amazingly gifted and committed in sharing the news of God's grace to those they are called to serve in Christ's name. However, so many are struggling to remember that God's grace applies to them as well. This is clearly a universal problem for so many Christians in whatever vocation they find themselves. Christians can become so selfless in their service to others, or so focused on just one aspect of their vocation, that they ignore their own needs of body, mind, and soul. This can lead to a de-energized and unhealthy life. They disregard balance. Their energy for service seems never to get replenished. At the same time, they neglect the gift of God's love and forgiveness in Christ, the gift that truly brings them healing, renewing, and reenergizing.

God's grace is *green*—the most renewable energy source available in his creation. He extends it to us over and over again in his dearly beloved Son.

For at least the last 50 years, in both the U.S. and around the world, the workforce is experiencing expanding rates of burnout and job loss in numerous vocations. The challenges of body, mind, and soul in church work and in so many other professions are staggering and unremitting. God is surely present. Yet the breakdown in vitality and wellness, I believe, comes most often when Christians believe they can do it all on their own fuel, consuming personal health, family resources, and personal relationships in the process. Is not God's grace—his love and forgiveness through Jesus—just as available as is the oxygen he gives us for life? When we don't live within God's breath of grace, nothing remains in our tank for resilient fuel. Fire cannot flame without oxygen, nor can it ignite without a source of fuel.

What I saw happening to church workers in particular troubled me so much that it compelled me to do something about it. So I gathered church worker care advocates from around the U.S. to meet on multiple occasions in the late 1990s to explore the collected wisdom and knowledge of how to stem this tide. Out of those gatherings emerged Grace Place Wellness Ministries (GPWM). Grace Place Wellness Ministries is a retreat-based care and education-focused ministry aimed at stemming burnout through deepening time in God's Word, wellness education and practice, and ongoing fellowship and accountability. As of this writing, we have taken more than 8,000 professional church workers—and their spouses—through this wellness education. My denominational affiliation is with the Lutheran Church—Missouri Synod (LCMS) and I have dealt most often with those who work in the LCMS. But what I have learned through GPWM can be applied to every member of the body of Christ. For more information on this ministry organization, visit www. graceplacewellness.org.

This book is a compilation of renewable energy practices, in every sense gifts from God, that have worked to bring greater wellness of body, mind, and soul to church workers and greater vitality and energy to their service. First and foremost, our energy comes from our Baptismal relationship to Jesus. But I believe the health, wellness, and wholeness insights presented here are applicable to all people of faith and in all vocations. My prayer is that there will be components and aspects of my observations of my own and others' wellness journeys that you might find helpful in yours.

I invite you to walk with me through these reflections and encouragements as we explore the importance and benefits of balancing wellness of body, mind, and soul and renewing our energy so that we all might be better equipped to live for and serve our Savior Jesus Christ. Furthermore, we want that living and serving of our Lord to be filled with joy, vibrancy, and longevity. Consider the words on these pages my prescription to you for embracing renewable energy for your Christian life and vocational wellness as you serve the Lord and care for his people.

Dr. John D. Eckrich

CHAPTER

01

RENEWABLE ENERGY WELLNESS

*"As a prisoner for the Lord, then, I urge you to live a life worthy of
the calling you have received. Be completely humble and gentle;
be patient, bearing with one another in love. Make every effort
to keep the unity of the Spirit through the bond of peace. There
is one body and one Spirit—just as you were called to one hope
when you were called—one Lord, one faith, one baptism; one
God and Father of all, who is over all and through all and in all.
But to each of us grace has been given as Christ apportioned it."*

EPHESIANS 4:1-7

recall a very poignant Sunday morning, just after church, when I was
approached by the wife of one of our congregation's youth ministers who
asked in desperation, "Will you please take a look at him? He's exhausted.
There's something really wrong with him!"

An immediate visit to my nearby medical office revealed a diligent
servant of Christ whose human fuel cells were obviously spent. He had used
them all up fulfilling innumerable expectations—many self-induced, and

many applied by the parish. Some demands and requests were appropriate, and many others that were probably not so immediate or urgent in nature were stressing him simply because he felt he could not say "no" or "not right now." Yes, he was experiencing physical symptoms and real disease, but he was also in emotional meltdown. His overachieving efforts were injuring his family relationships, and at their foundation, I think were damaging his spirit and robbing his joy. He was simply and completely *out of balance.* He had no energy left for his family, and no fuel in the tank for ministry. He had not taken the time to incorporate energy-renewing, healthy life practices (indeed, gifts of the Spirit) which could provide *resilience* within his daily living and ministry service. I believe, for multiple reasons, he had neglected wellness practices to replenish his energy that were *worthy of his calling.*

Yet, Ephesians 4:7, God gives grace apportioned to our needs. We are not to lose hope. We are still his, still loved, still forgiven.

Sound familiar? That experience crystallized my interest and passion to walk alongside professional church workers and their parishioners, helping to lift their arms and hearts in their service to Christ by encouraging vocation-worthy wellness. Being well, as I understand our life as a new creation in Christ (2 Corinthians 5:17), is not a self-centered process, but is a grace-filled, grace-motivated, grace-thankful, and yes, *vocation-worthy* response to what Christ has bought for us with his bitter suffering and death. Wellness is first and foremost a gift of the one God and Father of us all, the one Lord, the one Spirit, the one Faith and the one Baptism.

To reiterate, I am not the healer, especially of self. "For I am the Lord, who heals you," God tells us in Exodus 15:26. My faith assures me that I am not worthy on my own merit or deeds to receive God's gift of grace and healing. Rather, I understand my wellness as a gift of my Baptism, empowered by the continual presence of the Holy Spirit, working in and maturing my faith. I am invited then, by the Holy Spirit, to live a *worthy wellness* in my practical daily life as I continue to work out the purposes for which Christ has purchased me.

Let me punctuate wellness with a touch of medical science. From a physical standpoint, all humans require three core ingredients for life: oxygen, water, and fuel. God has provided for all these resources to be renewable in his magnificent creation. We can exist for about three minutes without oxygen. Without it, our body begins the process of irreversibly dying. We can make it a bit longer (three days) without water, and then our downward spiral begins, even with oxygen in good supply. Finally, we actually can go roughly 21 days without fuel—food—before we begin to irreversibly fail.

Let's even look at these energy resources at the most basic cellular level. Every cell in the human body needs fuel to function properly. Every cell is a tiny package of productivity; it grows, moves, and performs housekeeping activity, and all those require energy. The common energy source for all cells is ATP (adenosine triphosphate) and the process by which nutrients are used to generate energy is called metabolism. In fact, our human metabolism is the rate-limiting step that determines the quality of health any person will experience. (Mark J. Donohue, "Cellular Energy and Mitochondrial ATP Production: A Primer." toxipedia.org. Accessed March 2, 2016.)

There are little organelles within each cell that act as tiny "powerhouses" for producing cellular energy (ATP), and they are the mitochondria. The human body has 100 trillion cells, all requiring energy. Some of the energy-producing enzyme reactions in cells require oxygen and other reactions do not. But the cell cannot remain functional without oxygen.

Water, the second core component for human life, flushes out toxins, carries oxygen and nutrients to cells and organs, aids in digestion, lubricates, regulates temperature, and helps us fight disease. All of these functions are critical to metabolism.

Furthermore, a person whose metabolism is functioning sub-optimally will see the exact opposite of health and wellness. They will drag mentally; slow physically; be far more susceptible to the attacks of bacteria, viruses, and toxins; and often seek stimulant energy boosters leading to further adverse effects on function.

If diminished metabolism continues, biochemical pathways and organ systems degrade, and eventually early aging and death ensue. Burnout.

We will examine water and fuel in later chapters of this book in more depth, but let's take a closer look at oxygen. When it comes to oxygen, this is an absolute critical, moment-to-moment requirement for human life. I would ask you to consider that God's grace—his undeserved love and forgiveness—is the oxygen for Christian life. We are hopelessly and eternally lost and separated from our Creator and condemned to death without God's gift of grace, brought to us through the suffering, death, and resurrection of his Son, Jesus Christ. Grace is what God breathes into us at Baptism. As I said in the Introduction, God's grace is *green*—endlessly present, available, and renewable to his children.

What I saw in my practice, especially among church workers, was that they were very good at proclaiming the good news of God's grace through his Son to us in the church pew. I recognized that they were firmly committed to helping people breathe in this "oxygen" of God in Word and Sacrament. The problem that I observed was that they too often failed to breathe in that grace themselves, or trust that it was readily available to them as well as their parishioners.

This is crucial for us, whether in church work or in our general professions and jobs, to remember as well. Although God has, indeed, set us *all* apart for special service, we are still human, with all the foibles, needs, and limitations of humanity. We all have fallen short of God's glory. Baptized, we are all still saint and sinner. We all need God's grace every day, every hour, and every minute.

In addition to letting God's grace flow through us, we also need to take good care of ourselves. We need water and we need fuel to replenish our human vitality. We need to live a life worthy of his calling. I like to think of renewing depleted sources of water and fuel as "preventative" care. Though regular tests and screenings can be valuable, one of the best types of preventative care is *changing health behavior*, such as avoiding known insulting agents (alcohol, illegal drugs, cigarettes, and relationship-injuring addictions like pornography, for example), maintaining good nutrition, exercising regularly, and getting appropriate rest. We can apply these health strategies and skills both outside and inside the faith community.

Complementing and responding to the essential faith-filled relationship to God and what he does within us in Christ, what all of us need to live and serve well is to change health choices and behavior. We need to change the way we pay attention to the stores of fuel we receive from God as gifts to maintain our energy. The ability to change flows solely from God's grace through Christ and our faith in him.

Additionally, there is sound Biblical foundation for caring for our bodies, these creations of God that are "fearfully and wonderfully made." (Psalm 139) Caring for our "temple of the Holy Spirit" (1 Corinthians 6:19) is a way to honor God, who gifted us with these bodies for a purpose to work and serve. (Philippians 1:23–24) After all, it was through the sacrifice of Christ's physical body that we were redeemed. (1 Peter 1:18–19) Ultimately, we profess the resurrection of the body. (1 Corinthians 15) Our bodies, when they are raised, will continue to be designed to give glory and praise to God forevermore.

Renewing depleted energy stores takes effort. Changing bad health behavior can be challenging and tiring. I know, I've tried, and so have you. We go to the words of the Lord in Matthew 11:27–30 for help:

"Are you tired? Worn out? Burned out on religion? Come to me. Get away with me, and you'll recover your life. I'll show you how to take a real rest. Walk with me and work with me—watch how I do it. Learn the unforced rhythms of grace. I won't lay anything heavy or ill-fitting on you. Keep company with me and you'll learn to live freely and lightly." (The Message)

So what is wellness? *Wellness is a grace-gift of God in Christ, inviting us to consciously steward body, mind, spirit and resources to his glory and service with vitality and joy.*

We need to find ways to get away, to be refitted for service and re-energized to carry the load with our Savior at our side for our ultimate wellbeing. Our Great Physician prescribes it to us! And we need to do what he says.

02

FINDING WELLNESS IN THE SCRIPTURES

Disciples on a Journey

Vocation-worthy wellness is a journey. It is not something that happens overnight. We need to continually look to our Lord for strength and courage along the way. I think the account of the Emmaus disciples gives us insight into how our Lord helps us find wellness, joy—and energy—on our way through life.

As Luke the physician records in his gospel (24:13–35), two disciples had experienced the tumultuous events that had taken place in Jerusalem over the past few days with the arrest, trial, crucifixion, and death of Jesus. They were returning to their home west of Jerusalem, a fairly arduous seven-mile walk up and down the Judean hills, unaware that Jesus had risen from the dead that very day. They were grieving the loss of the one in whom they had placed so much hope. When they began their journey home after Passover, a stranger suddenly joined them.

"Wow, you're deep in conversation; what are you talking about?" asks this fellow traveler.

They're probably taken aback. "How could you be a visitor to Jerusalem for this Passover and not have heard about what happened to Jesus of Nazareth, who was certainly a prophet? He lived right and taught with authority. In fact, we were pretty sure he was the long-awaited King, the Messiah for whom we all had been searching for so long."

"And on top of this," they say, "some women in our group were going to the tomb to anoint his body this morning, and his body was gone!"

The disappointment on their faces and their hearts is palpable.

So then this stranger starts to take them through a Bible study class, right there on the road home. He goes through all the Scriptures, pointing out a "plan" that God had promised from the beginning about his restoration of the world. This fascinates them. Just when things get good, the stranger acts as if he is going farther west from Emmaus. "Stay with us," they offer. "The day's almost done."

Jesus stays, and they fix a meal, and the stranger picks up the bread, as is custom, breaks it and offers a blessing, passing the bread to them. At that moment, "their eyes were opened and they recognized him, and he disappeared from their sight." (Luke 24:31) Could they believe what they had just heard and seen? Was it possible? They ask each other, "Were not our hearts *burning* within us while he talked with us on the road and opened the Scriptures to us?" (Luke 24:32)

What has just happened in Emmaus? Christ himself exercises the bodies of these disciples in the arduous walk from Jerusalem. Then he shares with them rest and food to replenish their depleted stores. He works their minds in the curiosity he stirs about all that has happened in the holy city that week, then soothes their anxiety by connecting the promises of the prophets to the new creation he fulfills in himself. He kindles their souls as he opens the Word to them, and then ignites their hearts in the revelation of his true presence among them.

He moves them from distress to wellness, from dysfunction to function, from anxiety to peace, and from sadness to joy. Restored, refreshed, and renewed in body, mind, and spirit—re-energized—they return to the ministry of sharing the Gospel message. And so it should be for us.

As Christ's 21st-century disciples, we too "Emmaus-journey" in our faith. We hear Christ invite us to experience an abundant life on our earthly walk as well as in eternity (though that does not by any means imply that we will be free of all harm and ill here on earth). Also, we know we are called to serve the Lord with joy (again, that does not mean that our service will be without challenges, stress, and anxiety). The passage from Luke 12:22, "Were not our hearts *burning* within us?" is an expression of *wellbeing, of joy, of renewed energy.* The Emmaus residents recognize, perhaps for the very first time, that they are, as we are, invited to live in and serve our gracious Lord, as he opens himself to us in the Scriptures and empowers us with his Holy Spirit.

From Order to Disorder

Did God create the world to be well? Of course he did! Did he fill it with joy? Certainly. The description of his creation exemplified by the Garden and its occupants was the perfect picture of wellness. There was order: God, then man, then nature. There was ease: the Creator supplied every green plant and its seed for food. And there was joyful peace: Adam and Eve walked in the cool evening in perfect relationship with their Creator and with each other.

However, the Fall brings a drastic and fundamental change to the subsequent course of humankind and humanity's environment on this globe. *Order* is replaced by disorder. *Ease* succumbs to disease. *Peace* is supplanted by anxiety.

With the advent of disorder, disease and anxiety, we see the entrance of a redirection of God's good gifts of creation. Sin causes a perfect creation to go awry. As we look at creation gone awry, we detect a unifying theme to the disarray: in their disobedience, Adam and Eve constrict their relationship with their loving Creator. While they could walk unashamed and freely discuss all that they were experiencing with their Father in the cool of the day before their disobedience, now that they have ushered in sin and its consequences they feel the need to "hide from the Lord God among the trees of the Garden." (Genesis 3:8)

Constriction, narrowing, obstruction to free flow: these are fundamental alterations of virtually every physical, emotional, relational, financial—and, yes, spiritual malady of a fallen creation.

Constriction is the name of the game! Just consider a few common physical ailments such as heart disease, for example. Although God has revealed to us more and more intricacies of the dietary, infectious, and immune-regulated destructive pathways brought about by all sorts of environmental and genetic insults in heart disease, the fundamental factor that is occurring is a narrowing or constricting of the flow of blood and oxygen to a needy heart muscle. We see the same sort of narrowing in diseases like asthma, cancer, and diabetes.

The lack of wellbeing in the emotional life of the creature is characterized by constricted flow of communication, resulting in misperceptions of meaning, altered moods, and hurt feelings.

Relational woes abound when, in conflict, we try to fix the fault we perceive in the other person rather than focusing on our half of the relationship. When we don't grant others basic respect, our communication with them becomes severely narrowed.

Financially, when the availability of adequate resources to care for self and family is constricted, fiscal wellbeing is disrupted with many consequences, not the least of which often is the constriction of both lifestyle and generosity.

Ultimately, when we experience trauma in our connection to God, we find ourselves less likely to come to our Creator, to talk and walk freely and lightly with him, preferring to be harnessed to our own limiting strategies and approaches. When we have failed to regularly communicate with our God in prayer because of the constriction of sin, the Lord asks us the same questions he asked Adam and Eve: "Where are you? What have you done? Who've you been hangin' out with? What constriction has separated you, my beloved creation, from me, your Creator?"

The most descriptive 21st-century word that captures the essence of the effect of the constriction of sin upon the health of God's creatures is *fear*. The word *fear* is used nearly 500 times in the Scriptures. My quick perusal of a Bible concordance of the King James Version shows that a search for just the word *fear* turns up 471 references, and that doesn't even include the *fearest, feareth, fearful, fearfully, fearfulness*, and *fearing*! It must be a fairly important topic if our God devotes so much of his Word to it.

Jesus' ministry constantly addresses many fears. (Matthew 10:31; Luke 1:13, 30, 2:10, 5:10, 8:50; and John 12:15 to mention just a few) And in the Upper Room on Easter evening (John 20:19–21; Luke 24:37), his first greeting to the frightened disciples is "Peace be with you." (John 20:19) Christ died and was raised to rid the world of fear and to bring ultimate wellness to us all.

From Distress to Wellness

Rev. Dr. David Ludwig, pastor and clinical psychologist, has stated that the best modern word for original sin is the word *anxiety*. "If you are truly born without a relationship to God, you'd better be anxious! You're on your own, buddy!" Ludwig says. This is the condition in which Adam and Eve find themselves in the Garden after the Fall. And it is the condition we too find ourselves in when we are unable to extricate ourselves from the clutches of sin and a fallen creation—that is, until Christ rescues, restores, and heals us—making us well again.

At first blush, any discussion of the pursuit of wellness, theologically, needs to be placed in the context of our Savior's call to us in the Gospel to "take up your cross, and follow me." (Matthew 16:24) What is meant here is that we should surrender to him. We should give ourselves up to him. Our actual restoration (righteousness) is, for us, passive. Christ did the action. We do nothing ourselves to repair the schism between God and humanity. Christ did it once and for all. There is no call or demand for us to die again on the Cross. It doesn't do any good!

Sadly however, some feel, by their behavior or intention, that they must continuously suffer crucifixion again, somehow re-fulfilling God's Law. Thus this self-crucifixion becomes for them an integral part of their vocation and daily walk, and a part of their hope for salvation. In a deep part of their hearts, this can even lead to a sense of pride.

Let me sound one note loud and clear. Remember, that our entire plea for taking care of ourselves, not selfishly, but for the sake of those you are called to serve, originates for us *post-Baptism*. We understand that we are, in our Baptism, now new creations in Christ. We are saved, period. The work of justification is done. Now, through God's revelation of himself through the Word (his Son made flesh and sacrificed and risen), we can hear his Son's invitation for our wellbeing received and worked in us through the power of his Holy Spirit.

Therefore, now we hear Jesus say to us, "Come to me, all you who labor and are heavy laden, and I will give you rest." (Matthew 11:28) From our Baptism, he calls us to vocational wellness as he says, "Follow me, and I will make you become fishers of men." (Mark 1:17) We are invited to bear the fruit of the Spirit in daily life and service by having wellbeing in emotions, intellect, and relationships through "love, joy, peace, patience, kindness, goodness, faithfulness, gentleness and self-control." (Galatians 5:22–24)

Finally, St. Paul reminds us in Christ to "present your bodies as a living sacrifice, holy and pleasing to God; this is your spiritual worship." (Romans 12:1) All of these invitations to *practice wellness in body, mind, and spirit* dwell in the light of our Baptism and new life in Christ—calls of being well, serving well, living joyfully, and living with energy.

According to many secular health experts, there are five different areas of wellness, and if one area is overemphasized or undervalued, everything gets out of balance. The five areas of wellness are career, physical, financial, social, and community. Each element of wellbeing flows from a centering point of *me*—how am I well? (Tom Rath, Jim Harter, James K. Harter. *Wellbeing: The Five Essential Elements.* Washington, D.C.: Gallup Press, 2010)

Additionally, we have an all-encompassing skin that surrounds our overall wellness, a driving force that acts like an envelope, holding our entire wellbeing together and energizing our efforts at wellness. For all people questioned about wellness, this skin or envelope is our "mission statement" or for spiritual people, their "faith." Having faith—something outside of self, but fully integrated into our self—appears to be most valuable to achieving and maintaining wellness.

Christians, I believe, have a significantly different perspective on wellness.

As Christians, the very center of our wellness is *we*—meaning our relationship with God—not *me*. We are born into this world by nature broken, without a relationship to our Creator. Sin flaws us, constricts us, destroying the wellbeing and harmony of Eden. Sinful, and left on our own by sin, we organize and define the world and every way it affects *me* as if God does not exist. Consequently, we are constantly viewing our daily walk in this world as fraught with danger. We had better look out for *me*, as culture suggests. We are constantly anxious and anxiety abounds, uncontrolled and unending.

But, in Christ, our life has changed and changed for the best. We have a Christo-centric relationship beginning with our Baptism and/or our affirmation of faith. At our Baptism, we die to this old reality of "me-ness." We die to self. In fact, we are drowned in the water and Word of our Baptism, wherein Christ claims us and now lives within us. Truly, he is present all along our earthly journey, even proceeding within us to eternal life.

Each one of us is no longer a *me*, but now a *we*.

Therefore, the center of the wellbeing universe is *we*, rather than *me*. Our "*we*-ness" is defined by our vine-and-branch relationship with our Savior, Jesus. It is an intricate, fully dependent, Baptismally grafted, life-sustaining connection to Christ that is at the center of our wellbeing and salvation.

As saints and sinners, we continue to wrestle daily with the evils within and around us, but linked to Christ, we can receive forgiveness from him and put on a new self (Ephesian 4:24) day after day.

Furthermore, in the statements of our beliefs, as expressed in the various Creeds of the Christian faith, we proclaim our belief in the resurrection of the body, not just life of the soul eternal. We believe, in some form, that this body will be relieved, repaired, and perfectly healed. Our wellbeing will be made complete as Christ calls us to his side forever.

Does that mean that I can neglect or even trash this body-temple-shell, even as cracked and broken and flawed as it is now? Does God not care what I do to this vessel, as long as the wine inside, the soul, is sweet and pure? That is not what we read in the Scriptures.

St. Paul reminds us that this vessel, our bodies, are a "temple of the Holy Spirit" and this temple has been "received from God." (1 Corinthians 6:19) From our Baptism, we were "bought with a price" purchased by Christ. Furthermore, we are told to remember that this purchase by Christ of our wellbeing was done for a purpose. Therefore, we are to "glorify God" with all that is within us. (1 Corinthians 6:20) That doesn't sound like an invitation to neglect our bodies to me. That sounds like a call to wellness!

With this Christian understanding of *wellness,* we at Grace Place Wellness Ministries have adopted The Christian Wellness Wheel as a way to discuss and share *the practice of wellness* from a faith perspective:

Christian Wellness Wheel

The Christian wellness model has been the working format for wellness education at Grace Place Wellness Retreats for the past several years. The concepts in the wheel have arisen after many years of conversation within our faith community.

It has some similarities to wellness wheels developed by secular surveys and researchers. However, you will see several fundamental differences from those models in the Christian Wellness Wheel. Of note, the center of the Christian Wellness Wheel is our status as a "New Creation through Baptism." This reflects our "*we*-ness."

Baptismal Wellbeing: As baptized Christians, each one of us now is living as a child of God, a brother or sister of Christ. Therefore we look at wellness emanating from *we* (Christ within us) rather than *me*, which is what secular wellness models put in the middle. Our self-centered *me* tendencies are transformed by Christ into energy flowing outward toward loving God, self and others.

Let me pause and apply a second layer to wellness as we move our way around the Christian Wellness Wheel. I think there is also value in applying the well-known fruits of the Spirit from Galatians 5:22–23 to the components of the wellness wheel. I thank Rev. Dr. David Ludwig, our Grace Place Wellness Retreat leader, for his thoughts on this application. The key word from the fruit of the Spirit for this center point of wellness in Baptism is Love.

I would ask you to now view the Christian Wellness Wheel in its *horizontal axis* or dimension, seeing the elements of wellbeing emanating from the center value of Baptismal Wellbeing. It can be called *active wellness,* in that God invites us to participate in these areas of wellbeing. These elements of wellbeing describe how we relate to ourselves and to God's people, including all his creation. He has called us to *actively* care for self and others.

Vocational Wellbeing: We begin here on the wheel because, interestingly, career wellbeing seems to be a most important component of most people's wellness, primarily because it affects so many aspects of wellbeing. A person should be happy and satisfied with his or her vocation, so it is important to understand our gifts and passions. That does not mean that everything about our work must be peaches and cream. But one must feel productive, qualified, purposeful, and fulfilled by his or her daily work.

Christian Wellness Wheel
FRUITS OF THE SPIRIT · GALATIANS 5:22-23

And we must be serving in accordance with God's *good* will and for the *good* of his creation. Our vocational energy extends outward into *gentle* and willing service.

Other studies, looking at which loss produced the most devastating and long-term trauma to people's lives, show the loss of vocation even beat loss of spouse as having a long-term negative effect on health and wellness. (*Washington Post*, in reference to www.HuffingtonPost.com, May 7, 2012)

The key fruit of the Spirit words in this category are Goodness and Gentleness.

Physical Wellbeing: It is important to have physical wellbeing, although that does not mean living without disease. It means being able to cope and function physically at a reasonable level and to live with physical vibrancy, not being restricted in daily activity by significant physical limitations. We make health choices that care for this "temple of the Holy Spirit" well, focusing on what is good for *we* (our relationship with God and others) rather than just short-term choices satisfying to *me*.

The Spirit's word for this fruit in this arena is Self-Control.

Financial Wellbeing: We need enough income and financial resources to care for ourselves and our family; we need security. We should be in a fiscal position to not continuously be anxious about finances. Most important, we understand ourselves to be stewards of God's gifts of creation. As good stewards, we manage his gifts so we can be *generous* with all he has entrusted to us.

The Spirit's word for maintaining financial stability is Faithfulness.

Emotional Wellbeing: The key to emotional wellness is our understanding and ability to forgive as we have been forgiven. Forgiveness requires *balance*, balance of self-imposed and externally imposed expectations that are reasonable, a balance of stress and relief of stress, and a balance of workplace time and space and family time and space. It also requires a healthy awareness of the very real presence of Satan and his unending work to use personal and relational turbulence to destroy our joy, peace, and service to God.

The Spirit's best word for emotional wellbeing is Peace.

Intellectual Wellbeing: We need to maintain a continuous curiosity about all that surrounds us. We listen to, understand, and respond to others by seeking their thoughts in not only a non-anxious, but also a nonjudgmental fashion. We value continuous *study* of God's Word as well as the other gifts of intellect given to us by our Creator that add beauty and vibrancy to our lives—literature, art, music, and conversation.

The key fruit of the Spirit here is Kindness.

Relational Wellbeing: Relationships need stability, quality time, harmony, and peace—peace not just for the sake of avoiding turbulence, but for allying with fellow saints to build up the body of the faithful. As we make decisions within relationships, we allow for a full range of emotions. However, decisions should be informed—but not controlled by—our emotions. We know we only have power over half of a relationship, our own half. Our relationships, therefore, are exemplified by *trust, respect*, and *love*.

The key word from the fruit of the Spirit in this area is Patience.

Therefore these six elements of daily life make up the *horizontal* spokes of the wheel surrounding *we*.

Spiritual Wellbeing: Finally, the outer envelope of wellbeing is our faith. That faith is really our daily Baptismal walk as new creations in Christ—our faith-walk. Our walk is Gospel-motivated with our energy *flowing outward* into worship, service, and outreach.

Very simply, the key fruit of the Spirit for our faith-walk, our Emmaus walk, should be Joy. This journey in wellness encompasses our spiritual wellbeing, nurtured and empowered by the Holy Spirit. We need to have the words of that beloved spiritual song on a continuous loop in our minds: "I've got the joy, joy, joy, joy down in my heart!"

The Christian Wellness Wheel can also be viewed and understood as having a *vertical axis*. This axis or dimension is a reflection of how we relate to God, our Creator, Savior, and Preserver.

The center value of our new creation in Baptism (*we*) is directly tied to our daily Baptismal walk with Christ as *we*. This vertical axis is an expression of *passive* wellbeing. It is passive in that we do not accomplish this on our own, through our own means, but by Christ alone. This axis defines how we relate to our Creator and how the Creator relates to us.

Wellness from a Medical Perspective

I am happy to report that there is significant movement in 21st-century medicine to consider a much more holistic approach to a person's and a community's wellbeing, as opposed to the far more organ system–centric approach of the recent centuries. We have come to understand we are more than a collection of our diseases.

Don't get me wrong—a look at any reputable medical scientific journal will be filled with precise and detailed double-blind studies on the nitty-gritty of every interrelated enzyme interaction and genetic code felt to influence every conceivable ailment of humankind. But I can say even in my own medical education in the 1960s and '70s that there was a desire to approach the person as a whole creature. This perspective tries to integrate emotional, relational, physical, intellectual, spiritual, and even fiscal parameters to the expression of wellness or disease. Though there are still some detractors, of course, I believe for most healthcare personnel, holistic medicine is a form of healing that considers body, spirit, mind, and emotions all as integral to achieving the goal of optimal health. Perhaps the key word is *balance*. If one part of the matrix that makes up the human is not working properly, the other parts will be affected.

This balanced concept of wellness does not exclude the presence of disorder and disease. Wellness is best defined by good function deriving from paying attention to multiple elements of humanness. I believe whole wellness has several key tenets from a Christian perspective:

- God has created his creatures with innate healing capacity empowered by him.

- We are unique body-and-soul persons, not defined only by diseases that affect us.

- Health and healing are a team activity with God, us, and our doctors. God is essential and ultimate. We, serving as our own health advocates, complemented by trained health professionals and prayer, work with a variety of health disciplines to optimize maximum function.

- When imbalance occurs with resultant discomfort and dysfunction, treatment involves fixing the root cause of distress, not just alleviating the symptoms.

- Wellness allows us to live and serve with vibrancy and joy.

- Because Christ dwells within us, we can sing "It is well."

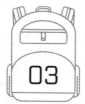

03

BALANCING WELLNESS OF BODY, MIND, AND SOUL

Ruth is one of those types of Christian educators whom faith communities hold in high regard. She is committed to her students and their families and willing to handle the challenging kids and difficult assignments for the school staff, lead innovative educational programs, and encourage fellow faculty initiatives. She is also one of my first patients.

Over the years of her teaching ministry, she had gradually put on substantial weight, had dips although no lasting episodes of depression, and a few significant medical concerns like adult onset diabetes, hypertension, and arthritis.

When I saw her six months ago, we had a heart-to-heart. Her blood sugars were very high, her blood pressure was unstable, and her knees were killing her. Trying to do all things, she had actually started to skip her beloved morning devotions just to get to the classroom early. I had to double her diabetes medicines, add another blood pressure pill, and have her start more regular use of anti-inflammatories—all this in addition to extensive discussions of a more strict diabetic diet, urging weight loss and beginning in earnest an exercise program. We found we could use wellness points from her insurer to sign up for sessions in water aerobics at the YMCA, but she had to initiate the project. Ruth had to make health choices.

Six months later, she reaped the benefits of making good choices. Her weight was down 21 pounds (two dress sizes, ladies!), her blood pressure was 122/80, she climbed up on the exam table without a wince, and she had a beaming smile on her face. Her scholastic workload and family responsibilities really had not changed, but she brought her life into balance, replenishing diminished energy stores by good health activities. And, most important, she returned to daily time in the Word.

With the Christian Wellness Wheel in mind, one of the best ways I have found to maintain energy and achieve wellness is to focus on *balancing* body, mind, and soul wellness activities. It is helpful to think of yourself running through the turbulence of a crowded airline terminal heading to your flight. You have heavy luggage (life, family, ministry) that you are responsible for and want to move with you. You travel more efficiently and more "easily" when you balance these heavy loads on each side of your personage.

God gives us a "temple" to house our body, mind, and soul. When we in our Christian lives balance wellness in all three areas, we keep that "house" running smoothly and efficiently as we give honor to Christ. The basis for this approach comes from Scripture in the words of the Greatest Commandment: "You shall love the Lord your God with all your heart [that is, your body] and with all your soul and with all your mind." (Matthew 22:37) Jesus calls this the great and first commandment, so it is only fitting for us to use it as a framework for pursuing energetic wellness with the Lord.

Wellness of Body

As Christians, we need to find ways to steward this "temple of the Holy Spirit." To maintain the physical energy for our service to Christ and his children, we need to maintain vocation-worthy wellness of our bodies. I found many of my patients did not tend to take good care of their bodies because a great number tended to work in high-stress/low–physical activity jobs. Their work hours were often extremely irregular, involving frequent nighttime requirements. For many professions, working weekends is often a given, again as it is for most church professionals. They spend much of their time sitting. And in many workplaces, they are constantly in settings where they are tempted by food.

My colleagues at Grace Place Wellness, Rev. Dr. Darrell Zimmerman and his wife, Carol, live by these 12 words of advice for maintaining a good physique, which I have found helpful: "Walk like you're late. I don't eat that. Find an accountability partner." Think about it: short, sweet, and simple to remember. These are words to travel by on our way to wellness of body.

In addition, *find a doctor*. Get a physical done on a yearly basis, certainly after age 50. Have regular examinations and appropriate testing of your eyes, skin, heart, lungs, and GI tract (including cancer screening) as well as breast and prostate evaluations and foot exams. Don't forget your dental health, as we know many illnesses are triggered by poor dentition. Most health insurance plans now include coverage for regular health screenings.

Of course, eating correctly and taking part in regular exercise are not easy in our often overcommitted and unpredictable lives, but both are worth the effort in longevity and vitality.

Above all else, listen to your body. When pains or changes in bowel patterns happen or when new spots appear on your skin, get them checked out by your healthcare professional. Please do not let fear compromise your long-term wellness of body. I like to recommend to patients a "two-week rule." If you experience a non-urgent physical sign or symptom that lasts more than two weeks, get it checked out by a healthcare professional. Clearly, if you are experiencing chest pain, loss of movement or speech, for example, or urgent physical trauma, get to an ER, urgent care facility, or doctor's office as soon as possible.

Wellness of Mind

St. Paul writes in Romans 12:2: "Do not be conformed to this world, but be transformed by the renewal of your mind, that by testing you may discern what is the will of God, what is good and acceptable and perfect." The wellness of the intellectual mind is crucial to a Christian life.

Look for ways to "exercise" your mind. Reading for general growth and learning and pleasure is great intellectual exercise. Enrolling in "continuing education" programs can be very valuable to your intellectual wellness as well, both for personal development and improving your skill sets for employment through formalized educational coursework. In addition, the pursuit of other cultural activities, including music, art and literature and simple leisure activities like crossword puzzles, word searches, Sudoku, and card or board games all keep the neurons in the brain firing and connected.

Part of the wellness of the mind is having a healthy emotional life too. Unfortunately for many of us, we define our emotional life as one inundated with stress. Stress is a part of human life—and, in fact, a level of good stress is important for the human being to run efficiently and clear our life-plate of tasks sitting before us. It is the so-called bad stress that burns up our emotional fuel and can flip us over the canyon rim into the abyss. Time constraints, unreasonable expectations, family tensions and illnesses, personal health problems and financial difficulties, and certainly even the smallest changes in our status quo, can wreak havoc on our emotional health.

Bad stress produces unhealthy symptoms that are fairly easy for a physician to recognize, and perhaps even easier for your family or friends to see. For a self-check, consider whether you are excessively irritable, constantly angry, continually in a dark mood, or outright depressed. Or are you feeling anxious—that deep and pervading feeling of worry and uneasiness? Anxiety is a sense of doom accompanied by physical ailments like headaches, muscle and joint pain, stomach aches, and bowel changes. Other physical signs can include irregular heartbeats or skips, chest pains, dizziness or alterations in sleep patterns causing you to be too tired at all times or unable to get or to stay asleep.

If you are experiencing these symptoms, you have moved past good stress to bad, and you are most likely not experiencing wellness of mind. (See the appendix for a burnout inventory test to take—especially good for those who are in professional church ministries, but applicable to all professions. You might want to skip to appendix to review this inventory right now, and then return to the body of the text.)

Here are some suggestions for how to improve your wellness of mind that have been beneficial to me and my patients over the years:

Maintain Balance: Time management and appropriate scheduling of priorities provide us with the emotional resiliency to deal with the unexpected and true emergencies that are inevitable in life. Allow time for work, family, and personal enjoyment.

Set Boundaries and Realistic Expectations: Establish parameters of tasks that you will and will not do and then follow through with those set of guidelines. It is okay to say *no* sometimes. And it is important to engage in those things that are most in line with your abilities and passions and not to overcommit. Remember, too, that there are only 24 hours in the day. You cannot do it all. Be satisfied with your daily accomplishments, no matter how small, and don't beat yourself up when things don't go as planned or you are unable to complete what you set out to do in a day. There is always tomorrow.

Be Committed to Regular Rest: All of God's creation, especially those of us made in his image, must rest—that's you and me. We can't run on full throttle indefinitely. Emotionally, if we are unrested, we tend to be irritable, unsympathetic, frequent criers, and short-tempered. None of those emotional outbursts will enhance personal life, family relationships, or work. So it is of the utmost importance for your wellness of mind to get good sleep.

Set Time for a Sabbath Rest: Sabbath is a time of rest and respite, and I would actually differentiate this a bit from leisure. Sabbath and leisure share some characteristics. I would prefer to define Sabbath as a time for solitude in Jesus. It is meditative, quieting, songful, artful, and a valuable time to be in the Word. It can vary from week to week and time to time. But the model given to us by our Creator and his Son suggests to us that we need about one-seventh of the typical week to be in Sabbath. Sabbath is not just a time of avoiding work (for that can include leisure), but rather a special "God-time" integral to our wellness and Christian service to others. The most important of our many relationships always remains our relationship to our Savior. That Baptismal relationship allows us to glorify God and really helps us to do our daily service for him more effectively and with joy. Sabbath is truly *vocation worthy*.

Seek Accountability and Friends: We all need others as honest sounding boards to share what is on our minds and our hearts. Think of these individuals as a "wellness support team." You might need several modulations of these support teams. They can include your spouse and family, close friends, others in your same vocation from inside or outside of your own workplace or church. It is best to contract with the team members. That can be casual and informal, but it is often helpful to consider a formalized "wellness support team" with consistent constituents and regularly scheduled meetings. (See the appendix for a list of guidelines for these "wellness support teams"—good for any professions but especially important for those in church work.)

(Also see the appendix for a list of retreats and other resources for wellness of mind.)

Wellness of Soul

Of all the elements of vocation-worthy wellness, for Christians, the most important is the wellness of soul. So do you have an understanding of, and are you paying attention to, the wellness of your soul? As faithful Christians, we may have the feeling that things are "well with my soul" and everything is fine there, but that may be just the temptation that St. John warns about in Revelations 2:1–6:

"I know your deeds, your hard work and your perseverance. I know that you cannot tolerate wicked men, that you have tested those who claim to be apostles but are not, and have found them false. You have persevered and have endured hardships for my name, and have not grown weary. Yet I hold this against you: You have forsaken your first love. Remember the height from which you have fallen! Repent and do the things you did at first."

We can so often forget our continued need for forgiveness. We can so easily forget to love the Lord and love those we serve, and even fail to love our faith in Christ.

So how do you nurture your wellness of soul? Stay in the Word. Read your Bible on a regular basis, no matter how busy you are. Stay constant in prayer. Keep the lines of communication between you and God open at all times and in every place. As the Bible says, "Pray without ceasing." (1 Thessalonians 5:17) Attend worship regularly to receive the Sacrament of the Eucharist and to stay in touch with fellow brothers and sisters in Christ on this journey of wellness. Keep going to church, as the Bible says, "not neglecting to meet together, as is the habit of some, but encouraging one another, and all the more as you see the Day drawing near." (Hebrews 10:25)

If taking part in these activities has not been a part of your schedule lately, you must ask yourself in all honesty whether something is missing within your spiritual walk and relationship with God. Do you have an idea of how you might have come to this lack of wellness of soul? Most important, are you aware of what the Holy Spirit is freely and readily working within you? Are you actually upset about your relationship with God enough to consider a change in your spiritual life? Are you ready for change? Do you have an idea of resources to help you change, including a path forward? Do you have the energy and sustainability tools in place to help you continue what you begin? If so, then you may be interested in following some or all of disciplines of wellness of soul that have proven to be so very beneficial to all of God's people over the years and that we share in our Grace Place Wellness Retreats (see below).

Sometimes it's tough to figure out your spiritual direction, or lack thereof, without an outside source or spiritual friend. That can be a fellow Christian, a pastor, or a colleague at work, or it might even be a professional Christian counselor. This discovery exercise can be worth its weight in gold.

To improve your wellness of soul, you might wish to pursue Word-centered meditation, fasting, chanting, labyrinth walking, or journaling. All of these are empowered and enhanced when intricately coupled with time in God's Word, prayer, and worship. (See the appendix for guidelines on fasting, chanting, and prayer-centered exercise.)

However, you may have reservations about admitting to others that you are struggling with wellness of soul, even if you are a pastor or Christian educator; you are not alone, and this is remarkably common. Begin the search by consulting your own pastor. Additionally, there are wonderful certified and specially trained spiritual directors available through Spiritual Directors International. (www.sdiworld.org) This organization can connect you with individuals or groups, publications, retreats, and conferences all helpful for spiritual direction. They are sensitive to your needs and requests and will respect your privacy.

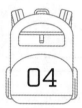

CHAPTER

04

THE BALANCED WELLNESS BACKPACK:
Life Practices to Renew Energy
for Christian Life and Service

The Holy Spirit bestows on us and empowers us with many gifts on our wellness journey. The Spirit provides us with resources to sustain and mature our faith, witness to and encourage our spirits, restore and renew our joy, and keep us healthy. The Spirit equips us with the elements we need to live abundantly, to serve effectively, and to love and glorify God with all our body, mind, and soul.

A helpful way to remember these energy-renewing provisions of *healthy life practices* is to visualize them as the contents of a balanced *Wellness Backpack* that we carry around with us in our life and service.

Therefore I present to you a Wellness Backpack that gathers these gifts of grace into a portable package that we as Christians have at our disposal at any time and place. Let's unpack each of the contents of our Wellness Backpack one by one. Let us understand the interrelatedness of all elements of our wellbeing. Let's appreciate the need for *balance* and the critical need for renewable energy.

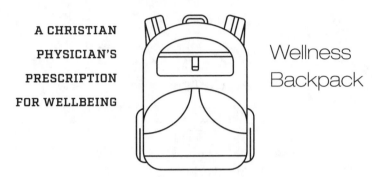

A CHRISTIAN PHYSICIAN'S PRESCRIPTION FOR WELLBEING

Wellness Backpack

The discussion of each individual wellness resource will have three components: background for the inclusion of that particular life practice in the backpack, devotional thoughts that can be used for further group or personal study, and practical suggestions for how to put that energy-renewing wellness resource into daily practice.

Enjoy the journey!

WATER BOTTLE

REPLENISHMENT THROUGH WORD, SACRAMENTS, AND WORSHIP

Background Information

We have already proclaimed that the quintessential need for all human beings is God's grace—love and forgiveness in Jesus. This is the oxygen of life.

After oxygen, water is the element that is the most important entity to sustain life on this planet. In fact, the human infant is actually about 75% water, roughly the water content of a good Idaho potato! (Neil Shubin.

The Universe Within: the Deep History of the Human Body. New York: 2013.) In our middle years, humans continue to be made predominantly of water (60% by weight). As we age, we get a bit drier; an elderly person dips down to about 55% water. Furthermore, we know our scientists are constantly looking at other heavenly structures to find places that could sustain life, certainly human life, by the presence of water.

So, indeed, we want to carry this life-liquid—H2O—throughout our human travels. For good health, the current suggestion from most physicians is that most of us ought to be following the 8 x 8 rule: 8 ounces of water 8 times per day (Mayo Clinic Proceedings). That recommendation has come into question recently, but it still remains an easy way to remember our need for water. Just as important, we need to remember that we are talking about eight ounces of fluid, not strictly limited to water. Other liquids do count.

The need to consume liquid H2O is a given. For the Wellness Backpack, however, I would suggest that we think about an additional type of water, the "spring of water welling up to eternal life," as Jesus describes himself to the woman at the well. (John 4:13) Here Jesus is talking about a leaping water fit for vigorous, abundant living. (John 10:10) This water will not leave us thirsty.

Our greatest human need is for the presence of Jesus, of his Word, to be continuously leaping within us, within every cell in our body, mind, and soul. Therefore to partake of the Sacraments of Baptism and the Eucharist (forgiveness of sins and means of grace) is essential, and to read, learn, and inwardly digest the Word is our daily need and joy.

To be filled and saturated with the Word—Jesus—should be for us Christians a given.

Modern technology allows us to carry the Scriptures with us, and scores of spiritual leaders encourage us to pray the Word as a part of our spiritual formation and sustenance. So God's Word becomes a most critical element to carry with us in this backpack. The activity of praying—and not just praying, but praying the Word of God—is a valuable resource for our wellness. We begin walking with the understanding that prayer itself is neither sacramental nor a means of God's good grace. However, many of our spiritual ancestors—and, of course, Christ himself (Matthew 6:9–13)—encourage our prayer, and especially encourage anchoring our prayer in God's Holy Word.

Devotional Thoughts

Let me share what I have found to be helpful to this practice of Word-saturated prayer or meditative prayer.

First, I offer you some thoughts on *being quiet.*

Setting aside the time to be quiet and in solitude for being in the Word is most helpful. We are challenged by two great temptations in 21st-century life: one is *noise* and the other is *hurry.*

We live in a time of constant noise. Much of it is *external* to us—media, electronics, audio and visual bombardment, multitasking challenges to our mind and body. Frankly, if your life is like mine, much of this external noise is unpleasant and disruptive to abundant living.

However, perhaps of more concern is the *internal* noise of our self-talk. I would ask, "Is that internal conversation usually pleasant and edifying?" Again, if you are like me, I do a pretty good job of beating myself senseless with should-haves, would-haves, and could-haves. Pretty often that involves words like *stupid, dumbbell, idiot* ... or worse. I would call that the devil's playground, the place where Satan establishes a deadly base of operations to attempt to separate us from our Savior.

Wouldn't it be healthier to find a corner of quiet, a cleft in the Rock of Ages, in which to see and hear God's voice?

Second, we are constantly in a hurry. Chief of sinners have I been in my life as a physician, husband, father, and friend. I love the quote from 19th-century counselor and analytical psychiatrist Carl Jung, who said, "Hurry is not of the devil; hurry is the devil." Jung was probably paraphrasing St. Jerome in the 4th century BC, "*Omnis festinatio ex parte diaboli est* (All haste is of the devil). Sad, but true. We are constantly multitasking or distractedly single-tasking our way through life.

Wouldn't it be healthier to find a moment of solitude, a time of deep breathing and slowing down, in which to see and hear God's voice?

We remember Elijah as he is exhausted after being chased by Jezebel (1 Kings 19:1–18) after destroying the prophets of Baal, and God calls him to a time and a place of rest and restoration and renewal. How does the Creator say he will come to Elijah? In a whisper! When it is noisy we cannot hear a whisper.

There are many wonderful Biblical invitations to a time of quiet and solitude. We remember Jesus' visit to his family friends Mary and Martha in the little town of Bethany, recorded only in Luke 10:38–42. Martha, probably the firstborn and probably a Type-A personality (sorry, Type-A's), was distracted by all the preparations that were on her checklist when Jesus was about to visit. In the midst of Martha's noise and hurriedness, she's looking around for that sister of hers, Mary. Where does she find that girl? Mary is sitting at the feet of the Word, Jesus, just listening and taking it all in. When Martha complains, Jesus validates Mary's discipline with the words "Martha, Martha, you are anxious and troubled about many things, but one thing is necessary. Mary has chosen the good portion, which will not be taken away from her." (Luke 10:41–42)

In another message from Scriptures, from the Sermon on the Mount, we hear from Christ as he gives us the Lord's Prayer in Matthew 6:5–14:

"And when you pray, do not be like the hypocrites; for they love to pray standing in the synagogues ... to be seen by men ... they have received their reward in full. But *when you pray, go into your room, close the door and pray to your Father who is unseen* ... for your Father knows what you need before you ask him. Then this is how you should pray: 'Our Father in heaven ... '"

Here Christ gives us a model that works so beautifully in the midst of quiet and solitude.

So pausing and quieting are important, helpful, and effective ways to come into God's presence as we enter a time in his Word, and a time of praying his Word.

Renewable Energy Practices

I like to think of setting aside time to saturate our prayer life by centering ourselves in Christ, by actually praying the Word of God, speaking in his language, and aligning ourselves with his will. This might be done best with a quiet and unhurried approach to God's Word.

The practice of meditating on God's Word has a significant history within the Christian faith. I would include Mary of Bethany sitting at the Lord's feet from the Scriptures as one example. Along the Emmaus journey of the Church, we have seen further models of meditative prayer in the *Origen* of St. Ambrose; *Lectio Divina* established by St. Augustine; Martin Luther's *Oratio, Meditatio, Tentatio*; and the second Vatican Council's recommendation of the renewed value of *Lectio Divina*, brought to a practical application through Contemplative Outreach under Father Thomas Keating.

Through our Grace Place Wellness Retreats, we offer Christ-centered meditation through a practice we call *Word-Saturated Meditation*. Let me share that form of prayer with you, with the hope that it might find value in your spiritual walk with the Savior.

Word-Saturated Meditation
QUIETING AND SLOWING DOWN

Begin: Choose a brief section of the Scriptures on which to meditate. Generally, merely a few verses from any chapter will suffice. You may choose them randomly, by just opening the Bible, or you may follow a prescribed sequence from a devotional guide or even a lectionary appropriate to the season.

Quieting: My suggestion is to begin by taking a few moments of quieting, breathing slowly and deeply (perhaps a five-count to breathe in, and a seven-count to breathe out). In doing this, your pulse and blood pressure reduce.

With a slowing or quieting of your body comes a quieting of your mind. You let go of the internal conversation, which can often be so distracting to meditating in the Word. Sometimes it is helpful to replace your own thoughts with a simple phrase such as "Lord [as you inhale], have mercy [as you exhale]." The use of a sacred word or phrase helps to quiet both your mind and soul, so that like Mary at Bethany, you can sit at Jesus' feet and listen to his Word.

By *pausing internal self-conversation*, you have the opportunity to *let go* of ingrained emotional response habits and behaviors, and rather, hear the power of God's Word within you. A healing and restructured emotional-response pattern can begin, but now directed by the Holy Spirit. We come to God's Word quietly and unhurriedly to hear his *whisper*, to open ourselves to the working of the Holy Spirit within our hearts, to understand God's goodwill for us as his beloved children.

1. Listening to the Word: As you are quieted, then offer a brief prayer inviting the Holy Spirit into your time of being in God's Word, asking that the Holy Spirit work God's Word and will within you. Theologians like Luther suggest reading the Word aloud so that it is heard not just by your heart, but also by your ears.

2. Discursive Meditation: Having quieted and received the Word of God, we now are speaking in God's own words, in his language, and doing so in the presence of the Holy Spirit. In this second phase of Word-Saturated Prayer, we discursively meditate on his Word. We can reflect on the entire text of the chosen passage, or even just a word or two of the scripture for the day. One might allow several minutes for this time of reflection in the presence of the Spirit.

3. Praying God's Will: Through the Spirit, God has worked his Word within us. However, we know that the forces of sin are also always present, tempting to separate us from the love of God. Therefore we begin a time of praying God's Word and will into our specific intentions, concerns, struggles—and yes indeed, our praise, thanks, and celebrations of life. Here we ask that God's will, as expressed in our meditation on his Word, be applied to our daily faith-walk, where we know that Satan, the desires of the world and our own flesh, will tempt us to try to separate us from our relationship with God.

4. Rest: We then take just a moment, in Part 4, to rest securely in the Word, being held in the arms of our Savior, the Good Shepherd. Being refreshed by being in God's holy Word, we may be guided back into the Scriptures for further reflection, or be released into the activities of our day.

On our retreats, we suggest three cycles of this prayer model: First, we read the entire chosen text for the day. Second, we focus on just a word or phrase from the text on which to reflect. Third, because we do this in a group setting, we take time to share our meditation with each other, to receive insight from those journeying with us. Often, we close the third cycle with the Lord's Prayer for our time of personal intention.

The entire direction and focus is to breathe in and within the Scriptures throughout the entire prayer, including adding a moment of rest as we prepare to return to a reading of God's Word. Our intention and direction is to invite God to work his Word within us, whether actively, as the Holy Spirit guides us during the time of quiet meditation, or passively, simply opening ourselves up to God to fill us with his presence. God is working; we are receiving. We eat, drink, and inwardly digest his messages of comfort, love, peace, and joy.

You can add a moment of reflective song to close your time of Word-saturated meditation. For many, that can be the singing of a verse or two of a familiar hymn, a Christian-based song, or even the use of a *chant*. (See the appendix for guidelines on chanting.)

There are many wonderful resources for reading and learning more about meditative prayer. I might suggest searching for *Oratio, Meditatio,* or *Tentatio* by Martin Luther, or searching for topics under *Contemplative Outreach*, and Father Thomas Keating. Finally, I would also examine multiple texts or articles exploring *Lectio Divina* by St. Augustine.

GPS DEVICE:

GUIDANCE FROM FAMILY

Background Information

Stars once guided seaworthy mariners and even the ancient Magi as they made their way to the Christ Child. In more recent times we had maps to mark our way. These days, travelers often carry all they need via satellite on their smartphone or carry a GPS or Global Positioning System device, which gives us location and travel time.

Although the Bible values our times of solitude, we know God frequently provides fellow travelers to assist us in navigating our wellness journey over the brambles and roadblocks that Satan, the world, and our own sinful flesh place before us. First and foremost, as Baptized children of God, our guide is his Holy Spirit. Additionally, we are gifted by God with flesh-and-blood cohorts outside of ourselves who can supply guidance, direction, and support along the roadway. These fellow travelers also share the time and space limitations of our universe with us.

Clearly God's presence and continuous work are made known to us in the Law and Gospel from the Holy Scripture. But I want to invite you to reflect one step further within the life parameters of a Christian pilgrimage, examining the fellow companions on our path (understanding their limitations as fellow sinners) who give not just orientation, but also supply accountability to our choices and behavior. These Christian brothers and sisters may caution us when we stray, and can model for us, in Christ, a way back to a pathway consistent with honoring God's will.

That GPS, I would suggest, comes for most of us in the institution of *family*. God creates family as one of his greatest gifts, even in the myriad forms that that family unit might come in these days. Stable, loving, grace-embracing relationships, especially relationships characterized by *agape* or unconditional love, are essential for our wellness journey. Family can mean those we are related to, but oftentimes can mean a close-knit group of coworkers, fellow church members, or just plain friends.

Why is family an essential resource for our wellness journey? I think it is critical because our family relationships provide energy, balance, and support. Life is tough and tiring. How often do we struggle to get home after vigorously burning our fuel in the workplace, whether that's as an office worker or as a family household manager, and are then restored and renewed by the safety, comfort, healing, and empowerment of our spouses, children, or close friends? Obviously there are healthy home environments in the family, and there also are challenging, maybe not-so-healthy interactions that are not as refreshing for all involved in the household. Under both circumstances, however, we experience interactions that can bless or detract from wellness. We get, in essence, home-schooled on wellness by our families.

Directional guidance from family works best when there are two essential components: 1) loving and caring relationships and 2) a significant element of peer accountability.

We learn different patterns of communication, trying and occasionally repeating strategies for conflict management, and hopefully gaining skills in bringing the healing voice of Christ to our family members as well as to those we are called to serve outside of our homes. In family, we have the chance to set and measure expectations, and we understand that we probably succeed at fulfilling those expectations best when we work as a group rather than alone. In family, we have a matrix of interdependent relationships that can implode in self-centered behavior, or work harmoniously and constructively to bless the world. Functional and dysfunctional relationships, however, can both teach us lessons invaluable to our service for the Lord.

A prime characteristic of healthy and whole living is that functional and productive behavior is more likely to be sustainable when it is supported by accountable community relationships, especially involving our family members. Those of us who have ever tried to alter health habits like smoking or overeating know it probably can't be accomplished without the efforts and assistance of our friends and family.

Devotional Thoughts

When we look in Scripture, we find functional as well as dysfunctional directional guidance within families. Rebekah guided her son Jacob to deceive his father, Isaac, to receive the blessing meant for Esau. Joseph's brothers decided to sell him into slavery in Egypt because they were jealous of the favoritism his father gave him. Eve convinced Adam to eat the fruit God had forbidden them to eat because she listened to the devil's lies. But we remember as well Aaron and Hur who supported their brother Moses in leading the children of Israel out of Egypt. We think of Mary who encouraged Jesus to help out at a wedding feast when they had no more wine. We consider John who took Mary home to live with him at the request of his dying friend Jesus.

We as members of a family need to be sure to give and receive advice to and from each other that is based in Christian values and Christlike care. "Let us consider how to stir up one another to love and good works, encouraging one another," the Bible says in Hebrews 10:24–25. Part of our wellness involves listening to our family members who have our best interests at heart. As the Bible says, "Put on then, as God's chosen ones, holy and beloved, compassionate hearts, kindness, humility, meekness and patience." (Colossians 3:12) Our ears need to be tuned to the voices of love from our family members who know us best and who are grounded in the faith.

Renewable Energy Practices

One tip for accomplishing guidance in the family is through family devotions. Family devotions mean gathering around the table at breakfast or supper for spiritual reflection. Family devotions provide a restoring "pause point" to both celebrate family and to do necessary work to move our families to wellness in the shadow of the cross of Christ. In my childhood home and with my own young children, this nightly visit was so important to connect all of us during at least a few moments each day. Using a devotional text gave us a Scripture verse, some commentary for thought, an opportunity for family discussion over a wide range of topics, and a format for prayer. (See the appendix for a list of devotional resources.)

This was an indispensable time. More than once, a profound Pandora's Box of emotional hot buttons, fears, struggles—and yes, reasons for joy—were opened in a safe and non-anxious space. Biblically based family devotions were truly a place to learn about life with our nearest and dearest. Here, our family truly focused on the *we* and, therefore, far less often on *me*.

Realizing again that our family units are so varied, opportunities for daily devotions can still be both accessible and crucial. In fact, even if your family unit consists of just yourself along with a connection to only more distant relatives or even faith community friends, there are numerous electronic means to connect to Christian chat rooms, blogs, and Internet conversations. Clearly, these sites need to be assessed as to quality, safety, integrity, content, and leadership. But many high-quality Christian web-based platforms are available and are helpful, especially if they are not merely used to "vent" feelings or unproductively deal with struggles.

Finally, since we do understand that all family life has ups and downs, it is important to recognize what aspects of living in family are renewing and refreshing, and what components of family are challenging and deflating. This realization provides us with the ability to celebrate what is working well and maximize our time and energy in those areas, as well as the ability to acknowledge aspects of our family life where we need to seek additional help, which could include further prayer, conversation, and occasionally even professional counseling. We can't move toward health until we identify the impediments to abundant living and serving.

GRANOLA BAR

STRENGTH FROM GOOD NUTRITION

Background Information

In addition to oxygen and water, we need fuel-supplied energy for our wellness journey. We need energy for a tightly knit body, mind, and soul. We are supplying this energy need best when we eat to live, rather than live to eat. Remember, the third element necessary to life is fuel—food.

As humans, to fuel ourselves in the best way, we should really be concerned about good quality nutrition that we can carry with us in our Wellness Backpack. Most of all, we need to make healthy choices in our nutritional intake.

It all comes down to choices. Here is the critical choice concept for wellness: *we need to make short-term choices consistent with long-term health objectives.* Think of the food choices made by Jacob and Esau in Genesis 25:27–34: Exhausted from being in the field, Esau chose to give up his birthright (a long-term healthy objective) in order to eat Jacob's bread and lentil soup (a short-term choice).

Generally, a good way to measure whether a food choice is good or bad is to ask yourself, "Am I feeding my body fuel that is good for *we* (me and my family's long-term and functional living and serving), or am I feeding it fuel that only satisfies *me* (my short-term tastes, desires, or cravings)?"

We make food choices in so many ways multiple times each day. Sometimes we're conscious about it and good at it, but sometimes we're not. Our long-term health goal should be to intentionally think about healthy nutritional behavior often enough for it to become simply a part of our natural eating habits.

Nutrition is such a hot topic throughout our culture these days with incessant talk, perpetual print, and unabated electronic energies being expended—let alone financial resources—to encourage better body-fuel behavior. Let me try to boil it down for you so you can make a few reasonable choices.

Here's the bad news: We are not good stewards, generally, of the gift of food and God's gift of the earth that supports food growth. Also, as it is turning out, we are not very good stewards of the environment given to us by a gracious Creator, including air, water, land, and its inhabitants. Half of the world's adults and two-thirds of the world's children go to bed hungry at night. We know that even if we are doing a partial fast, like consuming only water and fruit or vegetable juices, we are still eating more nutritiously than more than the 50% of the people in this country who consume large amounts of white flour, saturated fat, sodium, sugar, and processed foods.

But here's the good news: We can do something about it. Eat with awareness. Before each meal, thank the Creator for the gift of this food. As you eat, savor the flavors. Feel the texture of the food with your tongue. For fruits and vegetables, imagine the tree or plant they came from, contemplating the roots that went deep into the earth to nourish them, the water, sunlight, and soil that infused them with vitamins and minerals. Eat slowly. When you are done eating, relax and thank God again for the magnificent qualities of the digestive tract and the enzymes that break down the food to bring nourishment to our bodies. If you eat with this type of awareness, even once in a while, you will definitely think more about what you are putting in your mouth. In your desire to be a more responsible steward of the many types of food available in our grocery stores today, you will become more aware of what products to choose more often and which ones to avoid as much as you can.

Devotional Thoughts

When it comes to nutrition in the Bible, there are many schools of thought. In many instances, it seems that Scripture advocates a vegetarian diet (certainly from the time of Eden to the Flood, Genesis 1:29) though there are cases, of course, of the people of God eating red meat and fish. (after the Flood, Genesis 9:3–4) For insight into nutrition habits, we can turn to the miracle of the feeding of the 5,000 in which Jesus fed the entire crowd using just five loaves of bread and two fish. The people ate and were satisfied, the Bible says, and there were 12 baskets full of leftovers. The people apparently stopped eating when they were full, a good lesson for us to remember.

Also, it is helpful to recall that the bread of those loaves was probably unprocessed, whole grain, without high-fructose corn syrup additives. Keep it natural and keep it simple.

Another time when eating behavior is addressed in the Bible is in the story of the manna God provided in the desert. Except before the Sabbath, the children of Israel were not to save any manna for the next day, but were to eat only what they have been provided that day. This is a good reminder to us to eat what we have been given and not be greedy for more. If God's people did try to save the manna, the manna would spoil, which implies that we should eat foods while they are fresh.

The supreme instance of a meal in the Bible is the Lord's Supper in the upper room on the night before Jesus died. At this sacred meal, Jesus said, "Take, eat. Take, drink. This is my body. This is my blood given for you." The precious food of Holy Communion he served was given to the disciples and continues to be given to us as a gift from him. Thus, we are made aware that all food is a gift for which we should be thankful.

Renewable Energy Practices

- Wash your hands before you eat—there are germs and toxins out there, people!

- Eat breakfast. When we eat breakfast, we're far less likely to have raging hunger come back midday. Furthermore, the gastrointestinal tract enzymes tend to turn on in the morning and lessen in secretion as the day progresses toward night. Therefore, eating earlier in the day is more effective and efficient.

- Choose small portions and eat slowly. Relax and give digestive juices time to work.

- Eat at home and avoid fast food. We cook more healthfully at home, generally using less salt, sugar, and processed ingredients. There is no question that fast food is driving a significant portion of the escalating obesity rates (now up to 36% in our country), especially among our young people.

- Choose whole grains (whole wheat, steel cut oats, brown rice, quinoa, spelt).

- Choose colorful vegetables.

- Eat whole fruits rather than fruit juices, which often have high-sugar additives.

- Have nuts, seeds, beans, and other healthy, non-red meat sources of protein like fish and poultry.

- Use plant oils like olive and unsaturated vegetable oils for cooking.

- Limit refined grains like white rice, flour, and white pasta, and limit sweets.

- Limit potatoes, including fried or baked.

- Limit red meat to 4–5 ounces per day (the size of a flat hand or a deck of cards) and limit processed meats like bacon, ham, sausage, or salami to two thin slices per day. There is evidence of substantial increased risk of cancer with excessive intake of these products.

- Avoid reading or watching TV or dwelling on electronic devices while eating. These distractions cause you to eat unconsciously, generally leading you to consume more and enjoy it less.

- Control quantity consumption by using salad plates rather than larger dinner plates to set at your dining table. We have made this change in our own home with wonderful results.

- Consider eating a larger lunch and trying to diminish calorie intake in the evenings when you are less likely to burn energy and digestive enzymes are diminishing.

(See the appendix for guidelines on fasting.)

RUNNING SHOES

ENERGY FROM GOOD EXERCISE

Background Information

Among the remarkable aspects of God's creation is that everything within it is in motion. Every atom and molecule is vibrating and moving, even in inanimate objects. From the massive stars and planets of the universe to the most miniscule quark and spark of our own human cells, all has motion. That is our understanding of our almighty God: he is not static but in motion. That belief greatly separated Israel from most of their neighbors. God moved with them in the Ark of the Covenant, answered their prayers according to his will, and could alter his creation to help heal them. (Numbers 20:11; Exodus 16:31) He could even rescue them by separating the Red Sea. (Exodus 14:21) He sends (moves) his only Son from the heavens and anoints him to save his people. (Matthew 3:13–17) You can add your own wonderful "motion" stories to this list—they fill the Scriptures as God reveals himself to us.

From everything we know about our Savior, he was in motion from the manger to the cross, kicking swaddling clothes to shedding burial sheaths. Among other things, that was a part of his being God made flesh. If you have ever spent any time in the Holy Land, especially in Galilee, you can get a good feel for the amount of motion it takes to stride in that land, over the rocks and hills, rivers, and streams. Even "to go up to Jerusalem" is a lesson in movement up the steep slopes to the Temple Mount from the plains of the Jordan in the east or the shores of Mediterranean in the west.

God has created us to be in motion. It is a part of the way he made us, and he has made this remarkable body to have a heat and power source within it, to provide the energy for that motion. Furthermore, he gives us all we need to sustain that motion in his many gifts of oxygen, water, and food. Finally, he breathes within us life ... in motion.

I like to think of our proper and regular use of motion as the energy we expend to keep ourselves healthy and in service—that is, the proper use of exercise.

I don't think the Scriptures necessarily speak of exercise in the leisure sense that we often associate with that term today. My wife's dairy-farming family in Minnesota has a different sense of exercise than I do as a city boy. It is important for me—and for you, if you are a bit like me—to add a regular time of exercise as a part of our whole and healthy lives.

Our body-engine runs much more smoothly and efficiently when we move the components regularly. I would also suggest to you that our mind-engine (curiosity and study) and perhaps even our soul-engine (prayer in the Word) run better with exercise as well. After all, all of these parts of the human are interrelated and integrated.

So what types of exercise seem appropriate and effective for health? A bit of the answer depends on the specific goals of your exercise regimen. In general, physical exercise is defined as anything that makes you move your body and burn more calories.

Let's start with cardiac health. The American Heart Association addresses this under the category of preventing heart disease (which is the number-one killer in the U.S.) and stroke (the number-five killer). Their recommendation is to engage in 150 minutes per week of moderate exercise or 75 minutes per week of vigorous exercise. More simply stated, we should get about 30 minutes of exercise at least five times per week. That can be accomplished in 30-minute segments or even divided into 2–3 shorter segments each day.

We also know that even 20 minutes of exercise a day positively affects your mood and emotions.

In addition to regular oxygen-burning exercises (aerobic) like walking, jogging, swimming (wonderful for keeping stress down on joints) and biking, you should also complement that movement with stretching and strength training exercises for at least two days per week. The addition of stretching and strength training help overall stamina and flexibility, and may have substantial benefit to bone density.

Finally, it appears that regular exercise helps sustain weight loss. Alone, exercise does not necessarily cause us to lose weight unless it is coupled with cutting calories. But we begin exercise to develop its habit, and that then allows us to maintain the weight loss we have achieved through a good nutritional approach to our lifestyles.

Devotional Thoughts

We may not think about people in the Bible engaging in an exercise program. But when you come to think of it, they really did do a lot of walking. The people of Israel walked in the desert for 40 years on their way to the Promised Land. Mary and Joseph traveled from Nazareth to Bethlehem for the census and later to Egypt and Nazareth when Jesus' life was threatened. Jesus and his disciples walked from town and village to spread the Gospel message of salvation through preaching and healing and praying. The Emmaus disciples walked from Jerusalem to Emmaus after the events of Holy Week. These walking journeys remind us that those in the Bible walked with a purpose, a principle we should adopt as well in our exercise regimen.

In addition, we are told in the Bible that at the first Christmas, the shepherds "came with haste" to see the Baby Jesus, which is another way of saying they ran very fast—maybe the first 5K from the shepherds' fields to the manger. Then on Easter morning, the Bible says, Peter and John ran to the empty tomb. In each of these cases, running was something that was seen as a necessity and something that was done with joy and excitement, attitudes we should incorporate in our approach toward exercise.

Renewable Energy Practices

I have enclosed a very detailed, guided stretching program in the appendix of this text that you may choose to follow on a daily basis, or at least several times a week. The exercise regimen, which we lovingly refer to as Christians in Movement and Meditation, is directed at strengthening the body core. This program offers a wonderful opportunity to add reflection and meditation on the Scriptures as a part of your daily time of exercise. (See appendix.)

We know physiologically that the core muscles, which run along the entire spine and are linked integrally to the abdominal muscles and our extremities, keep us upright and help keep our internal organs in proper position and alignment, allowing critical organs like our heart, lungs, and gastrointestinal tract to function at capacity.

Here are just a few basics of exercise that I tell my patients:

- Always warm up the body. This can be accomplished with 2–3 minutes of marching in place, walking slowly on a treadmill, or just taking a quick walk around the block.

- Precede more aerobic exercise with stretching of ligaments and muscles. Ligaments connect muscles to bones and allow muscles to work efficiently so that we can move limbs without injury. Ligaments tend to become less elastic and more brittle with age, and, therefore, whatever we can do to maintain free and easy movement is beneficial.

Here is a very simple beginning exercise stretch routine I recommend:

- Begin by placing both arms above the head and meeting hands at the center. Then move both arms with fingers interlocked to the right, bending at the middle as the hands sweep downward, accomplishing a full circle as your body raises and arms circle to the left, and then again rise above your head. Do this five times to the right and then reverse directions, creating large rotating circles starting to the left.

- Then extend both hands outward, right arm to the right and left arm to the left. Create circles with the arms, increasing the diameters of the circles, and rotating them with a forward motion ten times. Then reverse with tight circles ever increasing the diameter.

- Finish stretching by separating legs about two feet apart, and extending both arms upward overhead, clasping hands, and bring the hands from the overhead position downward with the arms and hands sweeping between your spread legs. Repeat this motion 8–10 times.

This entire routine takes just a few minutes but has great dividends in avoiding injury to joints, ligaments, and muscles.

Additionally, for moderate weight training, you may use inexpensive weights, frúit and vegetable cans, or formal gymnastic equipment. Just as effective can be using your body's own weight and gravity to help with muscle strengthening. A simple push-up is perfect.

A final note on exercise timing: Many people like to exercise first thing in the morning because they feel if they can get it out of the way, they won't be tempted to use fatigue after work as an excuse to skip the gym. This is a reasonable approach and does seem to be a workable strategy. The only concern for morning exercise is if you are dealing with cardiac illness, you might wish to exercise later in the day, once the body has warmed up. Once again, all of us should initiate any vigorous movement with a few minutes of simple stretches and movements as noted above.

Note: In the appendix you will find the complete morning stretch and meditation package offered on Grace Place Wellness Retreats at www.graceplacewellness.org under *Christians in Movement and Meditation.* This program takes about 25 minutes to complete. The appendix carries the narrative for the exercise program. If you would like to see descriptive drawings which might help you understand the program better, please visit our website: www.graceplacewellness.org.

TRAVEL PILLOW

REJUVENATION FROM REST

Background Information

God modeled movement (work) and he modeled rest. And made in his image, we, his creatures, are called to rest. Our rest is to be in balance to our work in his kingdom. Our rest is a time of renewal, restoration, refreshment, and resetting of critical body, mind, and soul functions.

The invitation from God to rest is undeniable and is given because God knows it is critical for his creatures and, in fact, all of his creation. Israel had clear guidelines for resting the earth (Leviticus 25:2–7), as we are told, "The earth clearly is renewed by rest, or is exploited ruthlessly and finally turned into a desert." That becomes for Israel a part of their Levitical laws as *Shemita* or *Sheviit*, the Sabbatical Year identified in the Torah. During *Shemita*, which was the seventh year of a seven-year agricultural cycle, the land rested from planting and plowing and harvest, the produce was given freely, and all outstanding debt obligations were to be forgiven. Finally, the products of this rest-year were all to be consumed and no business was to be done with it.

The Psalms have recurrent invitations to rest. (Psalms 4:8, 23; 55:6; 127:2)

Jesus gives us additional models of rest, going off by himself, or with his friends, to recharge for ministry. (Mark 6:31–32) Incidentally, why should we look at Jesus' model of rest? Because he is the Son of God? Yes, precisely, because he is the Son and image of God, from eternity:

"He is the image of the invisible God, the firstborn over all creation. For by him all things were created; things in heaven and on earth, visible and invisible, whether thrones or powers or rulers or authorities; all things were created by him and for him. He is before all things, and in him all things hold together." (Colossians 1:15–17)

Certainly, the epistle writers also call us to this rest (see Philippians 4; 6–10 for example), most beautifully in Hebrews 4:9–11: "There remains, then a Sabbath-rest for the people of God; for anyone who enters God's rest also rests from his own work, just as God did from his. Let us, therefore, make every effort to enter that rest, so that no one will fall by following their example of disobedience."

Any farmer knows the enormous value of periodically allowing the land to rest and renew. The earth becomes far more fertile and productive that way.

So we, inhabitants of the earth, need this renewal too.

Let's try to understand what might be healthy rest and how much of it is needed by us as human beings.

Sabbath rest might be best defined as finding time to be in solitude with Jesus, or one-on-one time with the Lord. This involves getting away from the noise and hurry of life and placing ourselves intentionally at the foot of the Master. This could also include meditative prayer or other spiritual disciplines based in the Word, but the direction of the heart, mind, and body is always toward Jesus.

What about this idea of leisure? Is there a Biblical model of leisure? I have heard theologians say there is no talk of leisure in the Scriptures. Though I agree it is not clear, I don't think there is a Hebrew or Greek word in the Scriptures for leisure. In fact, the idea of leisure has become far more common since the Industrial Revolution, with innovations providing us with less necessary work time. I often wonder if the story of Jesus' visit to Mary and Martha at Bethany might give us a glimpse of a time when Jesus looked forward to relaxation and fellowship, although he never ignored a chance to teach or heal.

Leisure is an important part of our 21st-century lifestyle. But leisure too is a gift from the Lord, and I think in valuing it as such, we are to use this time as a means of healthy renewal, honoring that time-gift with wholesome purposes.

What about sleep? How much is necessary and how do we achieve the appropriate quantity and quality?

Most recent studies on sleep emphasize that we should make every effort to obtain 7–8 hours of sleep nightly. That applies to any age. Generally, we go through roughly 90- to 120-minute cycles of sleep from lighter levels (non-REM sleep) to the deeper, so-called REM sleep, standing for Rapid Eye Movement. As often as possible, we would like to drop into and stay in that healthy and healing REM sleep as long as possible.

There are three stages in the non-REM sleep and each lasts for 10–15 minutes, going from lightly closing your eyes, to slowing heart rate and lowering body temperature, to a deeper Stage 3. You have to travel between all of these to get to the goal of REM. It is important to go through all of these three non-REM stages because our body repairs and regrows tissues, strengthens the immune system, and actually builds up some of our muscles and bones during this period of sleep.

Devotional Thoughts

There are many instances of people in the Bible being rejuvenated from a period of sleep. When Jacob was on the run from his brother Esau, in fear for his life, he still took the time to rest with his head on a stone. During that sleep, he dreamed of a ladder to heaven with angels ascending and descending. He awoke blessing God, calling that place Bethel (meaning house of God), energized to continue on the journey God had in mind for him. In a similar way, when Joseph was concerned about his impending marriage to a pregnant Mary, he took the time to sleep and during that time of rest, the angel of the Lord came to him and told him that Mary would give birth to God's Son and that he should not be afraid to take Mary as his wife. Joseph awoke confident in his decision to marry Mary, which of course he did. Sleep can have the same effect of bringing about clarity for us in our decision-making and thus energizing us to carry on with God's plans for us.

We are reminded too, of course, of the time when Jesus was asleep in the stern of a boat while a fierce storm raged all around him. The disciples wondered aloud why Jesus was asleep at such a time as this. But Jesus assured them that there was no reason for them to be troubled. He calmed the storm, helping them to see that he still had everything under control. This episode reveals to us the importance that Jesus himself gave to sleep in his earthly life here, and makes it clear to us that our sleep should not be troubled by worry and concern because Jesus is always with us to take care of every unsettling situation.

Renewable Energy Practices

Here are just a few simple suggestions to help you sleep better at night:

- Try to go to bed the same time each evening and get up the same time each morning.

- Avoid naps during the day, no matter how tired you might feel. If you must nap, never stay asleep beyond 20 minutes.

- Avoid high-stress situations or exercise immediately before bedtime.

- Consider trying mind-quieting activities before going to bed such as prayer, reading, journaling, or gentle stretching. If you read to fall asleep, use LED lighting that does not emit significant UV rays.

- Keep your bedroom dark and use earplugs or an eye mask, if helpful.

- Keep your room temperature low. Depending on your tolerances, you sleep better when the bedroom temperature is between 62 and 68 degrees Fahrenheit. Your body goes into a "hibernation" mode, allowing better and deeper sleep.

- Don't consume alcohol immediately before bedtime. Caffeine use is controversial, and generally limit or avoid intake. There have been a few studies recently that suggest a low dose of caffeine before bed might assist sleep, so there may be individual variations with this product.

- If you can't sleep, go to another room or do a quiet upright activity like reading.

- Avoid prescription sleep aids unless used very temporarily and prescribed by a physician who should be completely aware of the quantity and frequency of your usage. Some people find benefits from taking 1–3 milligrams of melatonin and over-the-counter sleep aids, but again, please review this usage with your healthcare provider for monitoring.

TWO PENNIES

REWARDS OF GOOD FINANCIAL STEWARDSHIP

Background Information

"As he looked up, Jesus saw the rich putting their gifts into the temple treasury. He also saw a poor widow put in two small copper coins. 'I tell you the truth,' he said, 'this poor widow has put in more than all the others. All these people gave their gifts out of their wealth; but she out of her poverty put in all she had to live on.'" (Luke 21:1–4)

At whatever level you are being compensated, I think the Lord is saying that he is after your heart rather than your pocketbook. After all, everything is his! He expects us to be good stewards of what we have, and I believe he values a *generous* heart.

That is why I like to think of the financial wellness resource to carry in our Wellness Backpack as two pennies to symbolize an offering to the Lord rather than a wallet or checkbook or money bag. Our financial wellbeing depends more on how we allocate our fiscal blessings in service to the Lord and in caring for his people than on how much wealth we accumulate.

Certainly, on the wellness journey, one needs to have some type of fiscal resource in the pocket or the backpack to assist in obtaining goods or services from, well, Caesar. (Mark 12:17) The fact of life for all of us is that we need some type of currency to barter or trade for earthly items or services that we can't always carry in our pack, as self-sufficient and as planned as we may hope to be.

God entrusts us with things heavenly and earthly to be good stewards of his gifts, and to be working wisely and diligently with those gifts. (Matthew 25:20–21; Luke 12:42–46; Hebrews 13:5; Colossians 3:23; 1 Peter 4:10; Titus 1:7–9)

We are not to be anxious or worry over the need for these gifts, surely. (Matthew 6:5–34; Philippians 4:6–8) But as we receive them, we are to exercise good stewardship in their care.

We are to be *generous*.

Devotional Thoughts

The Parable of the Good Samaritan gives us a wonderful picture of a person who shared grace with someone in need, offering simple service in meaningful ways: "... and when he saw him, he took pity on him. He went to him and bandaged his wounds, pouring on oil and wine. Then he put the man on his own donkey, took him to an inn and took care of him. The next day he took out two silver coins and gave them to the innkeeper. 'Look after him,' he said, 'and when I return, I will reimburse you for any extra expense you may have.'" (Luke 10: 33–35)

The parable reminds us that we never know when God might put an opportunity to offer something of ourselves to someone in need. This Samaritan was on his way somewhere when he encountered the injured man by the side of the road. We need to always be ready to offer ourselves to people when the situation arises. In addition, this story helps us to see that it is the little things that we do that often matter the most. Just stopping at all to ask if someone needs help can mean the difference between life and death sometimes. What the Samaritan did was not rocket science. He bandaged wounds. He gave the man a ride. He put him up in a hotel (using two silver coins, if you notice). Be on the lookout for little things you can do or small ways you can provide. It doesn't need to be anything fancy or expensive.

Renewable Energy Practices

Let me comment, in general terms, on what might be some ways to assess where you are in terms of your financial health for your Wellness Backpack.

First, are you contented? Do financial struggles serve as a constant source of anxiety and interfere with your joy and vibrancy within your family or work life? Are finances a means of keeping score or measuring your success in life? If so, seek some professional and Christian-based assistance and counsel.

Second, are you eager to be a blessing, to be generous, no matter what your financial resources? If you find that you can meet your personal and family obligations and still give out of love and thanksgiving for God's goodness,

I think you can count yourself generous. If this intention or attitude about your financial health is contentious or threatening, seek some professional counsel. You are very far from the only person in that boat.

There are tremendous and readily available resources that can guide us in God-pleasing stewardship of the gifts God entrusts to our hearts. Let me suggest two: Brad Hewitt and James Moline's *Your New Money Mindset* and Dave Ramsey's *Financial Peace University (www.DaveRamsey.com)*.

One final thought about the two pennies you carry in your Wellness Backpack: An actual emergency you might come across on your journey may not be of your own doing. The emergency to which you apply your offering might be a needy neighbor. Having been responsible with the financial resources given to you by God's grace might then allow you to put his gift of grace on another in need, and isn't that exactly what you are to do with his grace—pass it on to others?

SMARTPHONE

CONNECTIONS WITH THE COMMUNITY

Background Information

The last element I would suggest you imagine yourself carrying with you in your Wellness Backpack is a smartphone to symbolize connecting with the community around you. It is important to our wellness to keep in contact with the people around us, to be engaged with others in activity. Taking part in "face time" conversation (not just on your phone, but in the flesh) keeps our minds sharp and our moods up. We are meant to be with people. God designed us that way. After creating Adam, God even said, "It's not good for man to be alone." (Genesis 2:18) So he made Eve and encouraged them to be fruitful and multiply—to form a community. Keeping in touch with a community of people in our neighborhood, church, school, or workplace is an integral part of being a Christian. We are called to share the Gospel with others, to gain insights from one another, to expand our horizons with the support of the people around us. Much like a smartphone, a community provides us with "apps" or applications for carrying out the principles of our faith that we have gleaned through prayer and Scripture.

The reason to consider this element as a part of our resources for our wellness journey is that we are called to serve the community and we serve as a part of a community. We are a link in a chain among many. We are equipped with special gifts and skills, but we need others to get the job done well. In other words, because we work as members of the body of Christ, we need solid relational skills to serve effectively. This in no way diminishes the power of the Holy Spirit within God's people. The Spirit is energizing and empowering all on the team; the Spirit works, guides, and inspires according to God's will.

But as with smartphones, too, communication can be challenging. There might be interference or a dropped connection or misinterpretations. But working through these challenges in a constructive manner is an essential part of moving forward in our wellness journey. Let's take an opportunity to look at one particular way of defining people's communication styles to help us connect better with those in our community. As Christian psychologist Rev. Dr. David Ludwig says, most people can be categorized as a *painter* or a *pointer*.

Some of us "paint a picture" as we attempt to express ourselves, what's on our mind, and what's in our heart. We search for words to clearly communicate our thoughts and emotions, and generally express those verbally with lots of color, details, body language, and often volume. In fact, Dr. Ludwig describes this type of approach as "thinking aloud." He feels that *painters* don't necessarily have a clear idea of what they are thinking until they actually verbalize it. They are trying to express a point, but it requires externally painting a picture filled with color and emotions. Do you know someone like that? Are you one or perhaps married to one?

On the other end of the communication spectrum are *pointers*. Pointers tend to work through their thoughts internally and generally silently. They process their thoughts almost entirely internally, and when they arrive at the conclusion of their thoughts, they then verbally express their "point." Pointers don't initially or easily express the emotional power of their thoughts without working more deeply and carefully toward emotional expressions. They do have emotion. However, it is frustrating to painters to not see emotions worn on shirtsleeves. Do you know a pointer? Are you one or perhaps married to one?

Identifying which one you are and which one the person you are working with is can go a long way to help in approaching projects appropriately and completing tasks effectively.

(See the appendix for a painter/pointer test to take to find out which one you are most like. Also see appendix for Wellness Support Team Guidelines.)

Devotional Thoughts

A relational strategy may be found in the model of constant curiosity that our Lord demonstrated throughout his ministry. Think of all the circumstances of those who came in contact with our Savior, where he was curious—even though we know he is the master of all people, thought, and interactions. We can learn a great deal about others simply by approaching people with the mindset of curiosity.

We recall Jesus being interrupted on his road to heal Jairus' daughter (and by the way, how often are our plans abruptly challenged by stressful requests from others?) by a woman who had been hemorrhaging for many years. (Luke 8:40–48) "Who touched me?" he said, as he felt this healing energy going out from him. That curiosity led to healing and a witness to the power of his Father.

We can reflect on his meeting of the woman at the well in John 4:4–42. What a revelation of the heart of God, as we see Jesus in conversation with a lone Samaritan woman, one of those "nobodies" who came to Jacob's well for water. She was a Samaritan, a Jewish race of people that the Jews vigorously rejected as having no relationship with the true Hebrew God, even though they were thought to be part of the remnant of the Jews released from Egypt to wander in the Sinai. Even more important, this woman was an outcast from her own community. She came to the well alone, when the well was accepted as the most important place of social interaction for the community. She was ostracized for being immoral, unmarried and living in sin with her sixth man. What a bankrupt life. What a "nobody" as defined by her culture.

But Jesus was curious about this "nobody." His curious questions drew her into a valuable and healing relationship with the Great Physician. Jesus expressed God's value and care for her; he honored her value, though not her sin, even though she clearly felt valueless. He gave her grace. He offered her the water of life, from which she would never thirst again. Jesus gave her water leaping and welling up within her to lead her to eternal life.

Jesus reveals to us that God values all his creation, and shows that we are to love and care for everyone, including our enemies. (John 4:7–9; Matthew 5:44) Jesus' demonstration of curiosity and love leads to his Gospel voice being heard in Samaria. "Many of the Samaritans from that town believed in him because of the woman's testimony," the Bible says. And because of his words many more became believers as he stayed and was in fellowship with them. (John 4:39–42)

The ability to manage conflict well is a crucial relational skill that Jesus demonstrated well for us too.

Even with his tough critics, and even though he knows all thoughts, in Matthew 9:1–8 the Lord engaged his adversaries and found a teaching moment with his questions to them. Additionally, he used this as a moment to heal the paralytic, and when the crowd saw this, "they were filled with awe; and they praised God." (Matthew 9:8) When we seek to learn more about one another, moments that could turn into times of conflict and upheaval can be turned into opportunities for effective growth.

Renewable Energy Practices

In relating to others in your community, I have found the *we*-focused approach to be most helpful and beneficial. *We* can ally with our neighbor and also bring the Lord into this conflict solution, remembering he is always with us and in us from our Baptism. *We* then ask the question, "How are *we* going to handle this situation?" We first develop the *we* by the way we use our understanding of communication styles ("Am I dealing with a painter or a pointer here?" for instance), then we approach the conflict with both curiosity and respect for our colleague's opinion. Finally, having formed a *we* and remembering that the good Lord is a part of this three-threaded strand, *we* can resolve our conflict by moving with our ally to a healthy solution.

Is this easy or quick? Usually not! However, the more we understand and listen to one another, the better we will be at communicating with one another.

CONCLUSION

Wellness Backpack
FOR YOUR CHRISTIAN JOURNEY

Now that you have packed all these *renewable energy practices* into your Wellness Backpack, and appreciated the value of balancing elements of health, you are ready to continue your wellness walk. You can approach your life and your vocation with confidence—and, God willing, renewed energy. After all, the Great Physician is with you and is the power supply.

Of course, health and wellness cannot happen overnight. It takes practice, time, dedication, and most of all, Jesus. Christian life and service are long-term journeys, not a three-hour tour. They are journeys that will last our lifetime, as long as we have breath on this earth.

But when our days on earth come to an end, the good news is that perfect wellness will be ours next to Christ in the glory of heaven, where, as Revelation 7:17 says to us, "The Lamb in the midst of the throne will be their shepherd, and he will guide them to springs of living water, and God will wipe away every tear from their eyes." There our energy is eternal. There we will find wellness with the Lord forevermore. There, it is well for my soul; it is well.

APPENDIX

BURNOUT INVENTORY

WELLNESS SUPPORT TEAM GUIDELINES

RETREATS AND OTHER RESOURCES FOR WELLNESS OF MIND

CHANTING GUIDELINES

FAMILY DEVOTIONAL RESOURCES

FASTING GUIDELINES

STRETCHING AND MEDITATION WORKOUT ROUTINE

PAINTER/POINTER COMMUNICATION TYPOGRAPHY SCALE

BIBLE STUDY GUIDE FOR SMALL GROUPS

BURNOUT INVENTORY

This simple inventory, developed by Rev. Roy M. Oswald for The Alban Institute years ago, has a proven track record for identifying those who are at high risk or already intently on their way to burnout. (Roy M. Oswald, *Clergy Self-Care*. Lanham, MD: Rowman & Littlefield, 1991, pp. 61–65.) I am sharing this excellent inventory with Pastor Oswald's permission. It is designed for clergy or Christian educators, but I think it has validity for almost any profession. More from Roy Oswald, Executive Director of the Center for EQ-HR Skills, can be found at www.eqhrcenter.org.

Clergy and Christian Educator Burnout Inventory

For each question, circle the number from 1 to 6 that best describes you. Then add all your answers for your total score.

The extent to which I am feeling negative or cynical about the people with whom I work (despairing of their ability to change and grow).

1	2	3	4	5	6

Optimistic about coworkers   Cynical about coworkers

The extent to which I have enthusiasm for my work (I enjoy my work and look forward to it eagerly).

1	2	3	4	5	6

High internal energy for my job   Loss of enthusiasm for my job

The extent to which I invest myself emotionally in my work.

| 1 | 2 | 3 | 4 | 5 | 6 |

Highly invested emotionally   Withdrawn and detached

The extent to which fatigue and irritation are part of my daily experience.

| 1 | 2 | 3 | 4 | 5 | 6 |

Cheerfulness, high energy much   Tired and irritated much of
of the time   the time

The extent to which my humor has a cynical, biting tone.

| 1 | 2 | 3 | 4 | 5 | 6 |

Humor reflects a positive joyful   Humor cynical and sarcastic
attitude

The extent to which I find myself spending less and less time with my coworkers.

| 1 | 2 | 3 | 4 | 5 | 6 |

Eager to be involved with   Increasingly withdrawn from
coworkers   coworkers

The extent to which I am becoming less flexible in my dealings with coworkers.

| 1 | 2 | 3 | 4 | 5 | 6 |

Remaining open   Becoming inflexible

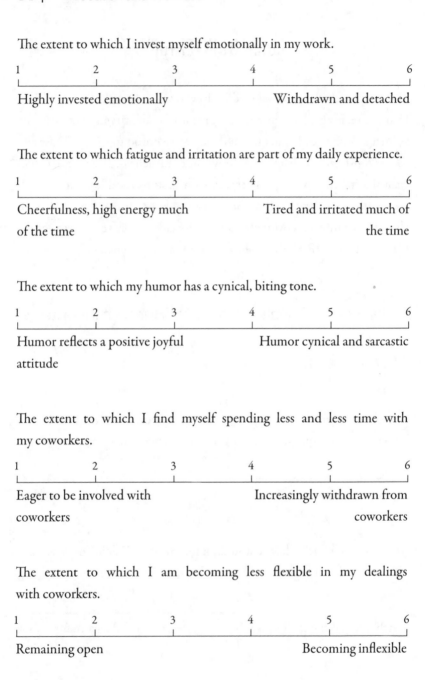

The extent to which I feel supported in my work.

| 1 | 2 | 3 | 4 | 5 | 6 |

Feeling fully supported   Feeling alone and isolated

The extent to which I find myself frustrated in my attempts to accomplish tasks important to me.

| 1 | 2 | 3 | 4 | 5 | 6 |

Reasonably successful in   Mainly frustrated in
accomplishing tasks   accomplished tasks

The extent to which I am invaded by sadness I can't explain.

| 1 | 2 | 3 | 4 | 5 | 6 |

Generally optimistic   Sad much of time

The extent to which I am suffering from physical complaints (e.g., aches, pains, headaches, lingering colds, etc.)

| 1 | 2 | 3 | 4 | 5 | 6 |

Feeling healthy most of the time   Constantly irritated by
physical ailments

The extent to which sexual activity seems more trouble than it is worth.

| 1 | 2 | 3 | 4 | 5 | 6 |

Sex is a high   Sexual activity interest is just
another responsibility

The extent to which I blame others for problems I encounter.

1	2	3	4	5	6

Minimal blaming or
scapegoating

Others are usually to blame for
the malaise I'm feeling

The extent to which I feel guilty about what is not happening at work or with coworkers.

1	2	3	4	5	6

Guilt free

Feeling guilty much of the time

The extent to which I am biding my time until retirement or a change of job.

1	2	3	4	5	6

Highly engaged in my work

Doing what I have to to get by

The extent to which I feel used up and spent.

1	2	3	4	5	6

High source of energy for
my work

Feeling empty and depleted

Total of numbers circled _____

0–32   Burnout not an issue

33–48   Bordering on burnout

49–64   Burnout a factor in your life

65–80   You are a victim of extreme burnout. Your life needs a radical change so you can regain your health and vitality.

Before going on, take a minute to fully absorb the meaning of your total score. If you have a score of 40 or less, burnout is not really a factor in your life and ministry. If your stress and strain scores are of concern to you, you may want to focus more on the self-care strategies that deal with stress.

If you have a score of 50 or more, I recommend that you take seriously the impact that burnout is having on your ministry and primary relationships. The following reflection questions may help you focus:

- Because burnout usually creeps up on us unawares, recall the times when you were not experiencing this condition. What changes took place in your life and/or work to help bring this about?

- What are some options that could help to alleviate the symptoms of burnout?

- Who are the individuals or resources you can turn to to help you reverse the burnout trends in your life?

WELLNESS SUPPORT TEAM GUIDELINES

First, if this is a support team for *you—you need to choose* people whom you are comfortable with, yet with a caveat that they will need to hold you accountable to your wellness goals.

Second, this team needs to meet regularly and also be available to meet spontaneously. It is helpful to have a guiding list of health activities mutually agreed to in advance and to be regularly reviewing these guideposts. Incidentally, if you are to share a "list" of accountability questions, the last of the questions should usually be, "Have you been absolutely honest about the answers you have given us?"

Third, this group may not always be static in terms of membership. Circumstances change, especially in mobile workforces. Furthermore, this group must agree to absolute *confidentiality*, because on unfortunate occasions, one of the members of the support team may inappropriately share something said in trust. Once that trust is broken, even though forgiveness might be offered and accepted, it may be at the point where a change of the team's membership is needed, especially if the subsequent emotional or relational wounds of this indiscretion fester for any length of time.

For clergy and teachers, the following resource used in congregations is valuable and is reprinted here with permission.

Church Worker Encouragement
(Mutual Care) Committee

For more information, contact Grace Place Wellness: www.graceplacewellness.org, John D. Eckrich, M.D.: jeckrich@graceplacewellness.org, or Rev. Dr. Darrell Zimmerman: dzimmerman@graceplacewellness.org.

As members of the body of Christ, we are invited to care lovingly for each other. "Love one another with brotherly affection. Outdo one another in showing honor." (Romans 12:10)

This certainly also pertains to the care of our church workers on the part of parishioners. Our pastors and teachers are continuous care-providers to us in the parish, 24/7/365. Yet who is mutually caring for them? We share with you some thoughts from different sources that might be helpful if you are pursuing the development of such a church worker advocacy group in your congregation. We thank Rev. Dr. Gary Schaper for his sentinel work in this support ministry.

LCMS-CMGS Wellness Action Team Report—
Church Worker Encouragement Committee
REV. DR. GARY SCHAPER, LCMS, OCTOBER 2008

A study was published in 2005 entitled "Pastors in Transition: Why Clergy Leave Local Church Ministry." This was part of *The Pulpit and Pew Project* at Duke University, Divinity School. The study received survey responses from 963 pastors who left the Presbyterian Church USA, the Lutheran Church—Missouri Synod, the Assemblies of God, the United Methodist Church, and the Evangelical Lutheran Church in America. Judicatory church executives were also surveyed for input. The purpose of the study was to find out the reasons for pastors leaving the ministry.

Also, the study notes that denominational officials "generally agreed that those pastors [leaving] tended to be loners in the district, for whatever reason not part of ministerial friendship groups or actions. They surmised that such individuals felt isolated." (p. 159)

From this study, a Presbyterian executive noted:

> "There are four things that I think somehow connect with why ministers leave, whether it's three years out, five years out, 25 years out. One is a changing context that they're ill-prepared to address, whether by seminary or continuing education. The second is what I call disappointment with God. Somehow their personal relationship with God has suffered in the process of becoming a visible servant leader. Then I think there's two other things: unrealized expectations, that is, I wanted to make a contribution, I wanted to help the world, I wanted to do something good, and I find myself running session meetings that argue about whether I go to one or two services in the fall. The fourth one is unrewarded vocation. I believe we live in a culture that has such low valuing of ministry and you really do sacrifice financially, and in esteem, and in lots of ways now that weren't true before. Two other things are lack of patience and an inability to disassociate from the congregation's anxieties." (p. 160)

A more recent 2012 study entitled "Predicting the Level of Pastor's Risk of Termination/Exit from the Church" (Spencer et al. *Pastoral Psych,* 2012, 61:85–98) notes two more causes explaining why pastors leave ministry early. First, pastors leave because of "Vision Conflict"—that is, they recognize and live a disparity between what they expected to happen in their Call and what happened in reality. Second, clergy (and teachers, we would add) develop "Compassion Fatigue." They become physically and emotionally exhausted from caring for others. This study and our experience at Grace Place Wellness confirm two potential solutions to these two challenges: Pastoral Support Teams, and better personal self-care and management.

Pastors have difficulty operating within the servant/leader paradox. The pastor is servant to the congregation and Word and Sacrament leader within the congregation. It takes a strong personality, good judgment, focused pragmatism, and solid theology to keep that paradox in perspective and to feel comfortable advocating for one's personal self. Any committee that is proposed needs to challenge the pastor to operate within the paradox, neither living solely on the servant side and never self-advocating and also not leading without a humble, servant attitude. The committee must not overly care for the pastor, which would mitigate against his leadership nor neglect the pastor, which would work against the sacrificial, servant attitude.

A committee that would challenge the pastor in ways that would promote personal health might be workable for both pastors and congregations. Such challenges should promote healthy body/mind/spirit attitudes and encourage the pastor to be assertive about his own self-care. In all likelihood the committee would end up not only challenging the pastor but also advocating for the pastor in those areas where further balance might be needed. The following proposal for local congregations reflects only the challenging side of the committee's work. Any advocacy would be a natural outcome.

Proposal for the local congregation:

Church Worker Encouragement Committee—a group to encourage:

Physical health

- Encourage and engage the pastor in physical activities
- Encourage or provide a gym membership for the pastor
- Encourage regular medical checkups and self-care

Spiritual growth

- Encourage a weekly study/share group with other pastors where the pastor is not the leader
- Pray for and with the pastor before the church service

Healthy connections for mental fitness

- Encourage socialization outside of congregational members
- Encourage activities and hobbies that take the pastor away from congregational worries
- Encourage the pastor's conference attendance

Personal financial stability

- Encourage seeking of financial advice
- Offer to connect a finance person with the pastor

A robust family life

- Encourage time off and vacations
- Encourage ongoing education for renewal
- Encourage the pastor's conference attendance
- Encourage ongoing education at a seminary or college
- Encourage personal coaching

Additional Thoughts on Wellness Support Teams from Grace Place Wellness

Candidates for the committee can be all or partially recruited by the pastor, with shared nominations by the church council, but all *must* be acceptable to the pastor. Candidates must keep confidentiality; this is essential. The membership might consider a rotating three-year term and should receive official appointment from the council. There should be regular, confidential reporting to the council. The pastor should draft the agenda where possible with the committee invited to add items brought to their attention. They should meet 4–5 times per year at a minimum. Further, the committee itself, with consultation from the pastor, church council, and outside resources like Grace Place Wellness, if desired, should prepare a document detailing the composition, scope, and structure of the committee and orient new members well.

Please note that if a church has a multi-pastor team ministry, it is best for each pastor to have his own support committee separate from other pastors' committees. This encourages confidentiality and effectiveness.

Finally, note that it is possible for congregations additionally to have church worker encouragement committees for their teaching staff as well as for their pastors. This does bring layers of complexity, especially with a large staff of a Lutheran school, and the congregation can consider a committee for the principal alone, or a general educational staff committee that could be related to the school board if separate from the church council.

Let Grace Place Wellness assist with more information: www.graceplacewellness.org.

RETREATS AND OTHER RESOURCES FOR WELLNESS OF MIND

Many denominations have retreat centers and retreat programming. Information can be found through your particular denomination's website.

Here are a few specific denomination retreat resources that I am aware of, which I highly recommend:

CREDO within the Episcopal faith is outstanding for Episcopal priests and is strongly encouraged: www.episcopalcredo.org. They also may have openings for other Christian clergy to participate in some of their programs.

Several Methodist resources are available for UMC members; visit their sites including www.umc.org and www.retreatfinder.com.

For Presbyterians, depending on your specific presbytery, a few sites are available, including zephyrpoint.org and www.pensions.org as well as calvincenter.net for PCUSA clergy.

United Church of Christ clergy can receive guidance through their conference, such as www.secucc.org for those in the Southeast Conference of the UCC, or at www.ucc.org.

Roman Catholic priests and parochial educators have numerous retreat and counseling opportunities generally through their archdiocese, but a few general resources might be www.jesuites.org, www.courageouspriest.com, and for general retreats, www.catholicretreats.net.

Within the Lutheran Church—Missouri Synod we have our own ministry to all church workers, Grace Place Wellness Ministries, www.graceplacewellness.org, and hold retreats all across the U.S. Generally, the Grace Place Wellness Retreats are open to all ordained or commissioned church workers, so this includes pastors, teachers, deacons and deaconesses, youth ministers or DCEs, ministers of music, missionaries, and their spouses. We find inclusion of spouses, if married, to be essential for balanced wellbeing.

The LCMS also has DOXOLOGY for clergy spiritual and counseling care at www.doxology.us.

For clergy/teachers currently experiencing burnout, an additional resource is Shepherd's Canyon: www.shepherdscanyonretreat.com.

Finally, a nondenominational resource for those needing vocational healing and restoration is Marble Retreat in Marble, CO: www.marbleretreat.org.

I know I may not have shared resources in your particular denomination, but these resources are easily available through your Internet access.

CHANTING GUIDELINES

I like the phrase "He who sings prays twice," to paraphrase St. Augustine of Hippo in A.D. 430 in reference to Ephesians 5:19 and Colossians 3:16.

I enjoy the spiritual discipline of chanting because chanting may be the perfect exercise balancing physical, emotional, intellectual, and spiritual elements of health. Chanting involves anchoring a few simple lines of Scripture, or a hymn verse, or a Scripture-based concise spiritual thought with song-sounds. The tune and text do, in fact, connect closely within our limbic system, where we understand much of our emotional/relational/ social awareness drives and thoughts reside. That's the science.

The singing of the song recalls the roots of our faith heritage, connecting our faith to our present circumstance and the presence of Christ within us and girding us for our future journey.

Here are a few tips on chanting:

- Chanting is best done for 15–30 minutes. However, any chance to chant is time well spent. For example, a drive to work or between appointments provides a terrific opportunity to sing an old, favorite hymn verse or a 2–3 line spiritual phrase. Turn the radio off and chant away! You might be amazed at how refreshed and calm you are as you approach an upcoming meeting or a doctor's appointment when you precede it with a particularly meaningful chant.

- Chant the lines to a particularly meaningful hymn, one that you have grown up with or that connects you to those special relationships with Christ planted in you by parents or family or your faith community. As a physician, I have had the extraordinary experience of being at the bedside of a sick child or a dying senior citizen, and listened to them sing a well-learned old hymn text or Sunday school song—a tune that reinforces for them the presence of the Good Shepherd and his leading them to calm waters, or that announces to the Lord their approaching and his welcome into his kingdom.

- Consider using a chant for your approach to the Lord's Table and reception of the Eucharist.

A list of chants for you to consider, which you can listen to in various forms on YouTube:

Jesus, Remember Me

Breathe on Me, Breath of God

Turn Your Eyes Upon Jesus

FAMILY DEVOTIONAL RESOURCES

Little Visits With God (still in print through Concordia Publishing House, St. Louis)

Portals of Prayer, www.cph.org

Our Daily Bread, www.odb.org

The Upper Room, devotional.upperroom.org

Living Faith: Daily Devotions for Catholics, www.livingfaith.com

Hope-Full Living: Daily Devotions for Seniors, www.hopefulldevotions.com

FASTING GUIDELINES

Fasting, coupled with prayer, exemplifies a Who's Who of the Scriptures: Moses (Exodus 34:28), Elijah (1 Kings 19), Hebrew Day of Atonement (Leviticus 16:31), King David (2 Samuel 12:16), Daniel (Daniel 1:8–14), Jesus (Matthew 4), and the early Disciples (Acts 13:2–3).

There are a few Biblical values linked to fasting, including repentance and contrition, concern for illness, celebrating religious events, and preparation for ministry.

Here are a few guidelines for how we should carry out a proper fast. They are suggestions, not laws!

- Always couple the fasting with prayer. Intentionally placing ourselves at the feet of our Savior unencumbered by distracting influences, noise, and hurry has great value to our body, mind, and soul. We place ourselves in God's arms for complete sustenance, no matter how long we choose to fast.

- This is a marvelous time to spend time in his Word. For example, when hunger reminds us of our earthly needs, this is a perfect opportunity to turn to Scripture and turn to the Lord to reveal his will to us in this prayer time.

- Set an objective or direction for your fast, relying on Biblical guidance. Is this a time for healing, guidance with struggles, spiritual renewal, or grace for a particularly stressing issue? Ask for the Holy Spirit's presence and work within your time of study of the Word and prayer.

- Determine the length of time you wish to fast. One meal, one day, three days, a week, and so on. If this is your first effort, begin slowly and gently.

- Determine the type of fast God is calling you to. Are you going to take water only? Or might you take water and fruit juices, or small amounts of light food, such as fruits or vegetables? These are all acceptable formats, depending on your medical history. For example, if you are diabetic, or have other significant digestive or cardiovascular illnesses, you may not want to take high quantities of direct sugar-loaded products like juice. And if diabetic, you need to monitor your blood sugars frequently. *Always* clear this activity with your primary care physician or health professional.

Prepare for your fast by doing some proactive work:

- No meat for 24 hours before the fast; fruits and vegetables for 12 hours before.

- Plenty of hydration.

- Confess your sins and accept God's forgiveness. (1 John 1:9) Seek forgiveness from those you know you have offended and forgive those who might have hurt you. (Mark 11:25; Luke 11:4) Make restitution as the Holy Spirit might lead you.

- Call upon the Holy Spirit to accompany your fasting journey. (1 John 5:14–15)

- Surrender to Jesus. (Romans 12:1–2)

- Meditate on the nature of God's love, power, wisdom, sovereignty, compassion, and grace. (Psalms 48:9–10, 103:1–8)

- Open your heart to God's goodness. (Hebrews 11:6)

- Remember, Satan is prowling about you and will put a target on your back to destroy your connection to God. (Galatians 5:16–17)

- Consider what physical or social activities you might want to avoid or restrict. It's probably not a great time to run a marathon. You should consider milder activities, however, like walking.

- Realize you might feel hunger pains, or even feel a bit fatigued or dizzy. Expect that, but if it becomes overwhelming, limit the time of your fast. Remember this is a grace activity, not a law activity.

- Check with your physician about taking your prescribed or over-the-counter medications. The doctor may recommend that you take some medications with a bit of food or a cracker to avoid gastric irritation (anti-inflammatory medications, for example).

- Identify regular times of prayer in the Word, as well as allowing for times of more spontaneous conversation with Jesus. This may also be a great time to journal your thoughts. Many find fasting to be a wonderful time of clarity and a chance to think more deeply about challenges and opportunities.

- Break your fast as gently as you began, slowly reintroducing lighter foods, like fruits and vegetables, and then expand your diet as appropriate within the first 24–48 hours.

STRETCHING AND MEDITATION WORKOUT ROUTINE

Christians in Movement and Meditation

Here is a detailed and guided stretching and meditation program we use each morning on Grace Place Wellness Retreats. It is a marvelous way to kick off each morning, again, coupled with a time of Morning Prayer or Scriptural devotions. Exercise to music—avoid music with lyrics but preferably find music that is soothing to you and carries simple melody lines. In the absence of lyrics, you are more easily led into focus on God's Word and the whisper of prayer.

Part 1

- Warm up: march or dance in place to upbeat music about 2–3 minutes.

- Deep breathing: belly out (inhale) and belly in (exhale). Do what I call a "body CAT scan," looking for indicators of tension spots in your body: neck, back, head, teeth. Breathe to the location of the tension, and as you exhale slowly, let the tension go.

- Active stretch: a.) large vertical circles with both arms together clockwise and counterclockwise; b.) chop with hands clasped above head and then swing between legs; c.) arm circles with increasing diameter clockwise and counterclockwise.

- Breathe in while taking hands/arms from side to straight above head, then exhale as you bring hands/arms down and cross in front of you. Repeat three times.

- Cleansing breath: belly out as you inhale, belly in as you exhale.

- Breathe in while taking hands/arms from side to above head, then fold body in half, extending fingertips to floor as you exhale.

Raise hands and body halfway up as you inhale, then exhale while bringing hands and fingertips back to floor. Finally, inhale, raising body up and spreading hands out to side and finally up overhead, then exhale while bringing hands to sides and then cross in front of body. Repeat entire motion three times.

- Cleansing breath: belly out, belly in.

- Inhale as you bring both hands together (but about one foot apart) up over head, then exhale as you swing hands downward past knees and extend hands up in air behind back. Inhale while bringing arms and body upward and repeat entire motion three times.

- Cleansing breath: belly out, belly in.

- Grab right arm between elbow and shoulder with left hand and swing right arm around so that shoulder is stretched and right arm and hand are extended behind left side of body. Repeat using right hand to grasp left arm and extend left arm behind right side of body. Repeat all three times.

- Drop chin to chest. Move head to left, back, right, and forward positions three times. Note: Be sure to hit those targets rather than rotating neck, which could cause neck problems. Reverse directions and repeat three times.

- Then move motion to waist and rotate like a hula-hooping motion clockwise three times and then counterclockwise three times.

- Rub hands together to create warmth and friction, then bend over and place warmed hands on knees and rotate on ankles clockwise three times and counterclockwise three times.

Part 2

- Use hands to gently help yourself down to the sitting position and sit cross-legged, if possible. Sit with your back straight (you might even use a pillow under your rear end to straighten your back). Take some deep breaths.

- Lift right arm, circulate right hand to increase blood flow. Then take a big breath in, then as you exhale, stretch right arm and hand over head and all the way out to the left, getting as close as possible to the left-side floor. Repeat this three times, making sure your hand and arm go directly overhead rather than in front of body. Repeat three times using the left arm.

- Stretch legs in front of you and as you exhale; stretch your arms and hands to touch your toes (or there about). Take long, slow stretch, trying to keep knees flat on surface.

- Lift right leg over left, bent at knee, and place right foot flat on ground to the left of left leg. As you do this, twist the body so that the left hand and arm are placed behind the body on the left side and stretched all the way back. Look out over the left hand. Repeat the process, now using the left leg over the right leg and the right arm/hand stretched to the right side of the body—look out over the right hand.

- Lie flat on your back. Lift legs and do ten scissor-kicks or stretches, once above then one below. Count out loud to ten. Drop legs down to breathe and rest. Repeat the ten count a total of three repetitions.

- Lying on your back, pick up right leg, bend at knee, and then grasp right shin with both hands. Rotate right hip and legs clockwise and counterclockwise three times. Again, flat on your back with hands on right shin, take a deep breath in with hands on the floor; exhale as you raise head to bent right knee. Inhale while moving head back to the floor. Repeat one time. Then grasp bent right knee with left hand and pull right knee and leg across body out to the left side. Extend right hand out to right side and look out over right hand. Then grasp right knee with right hand and stretch right knee out to right side, simultaneously stretching left hand out to left and looking over left hand. Bring right knee to center and grasp shin with both hands. With head flat on the floor, inhale. As you then exhale, bring right knee and head together. Then inhale and move head to floor. Drop right leg down flat and rest for just a moment. Then repeat and mirror entire process with the left leg bent and hands on left shin.

- Roll body to right side. Bring knees up to fetal position for balance and extend left hand on top of right all the way to right side. The left hand will act like the second hand of a clock. First rotate the hand above your head in an even plane level with the ground as you are inhaling. As your left hand is extended out to the 3 o'clock/9 o'clock position, both shoulder blades should be flat against the ground. Then continue rotation as you exhale, allowing left hand to sweep across the lower body and knees and finally come together at the right hand. Repeat this motion a total of three times.

- Now, lying in the same position, left hand on right, let the left hand sweep up the right arm, across the chest, and extend all the way to the left as you inhale. You should find your shoulder blades flat with lower body still lying on the right side. Exhale and you let your left arm/hand reach up to ceiling and then come back to original position on top of right hand. Repeat a total of three times.

- Flip body over to lie on left side and repeat entire routine with now the right hand acting as the second hand of the clock, inhaling on upper half and exhaling on lower half. Repeat three times. Then also do the right hand sweep up the left arm and out to the right side (shoulder blades flat), then reaching to the ceiling and coming together to the left side. Repeat three times.

- Lie in prone position (lying on your stomach) and rest a moment.

Part 3

- From the prone position, use your hands to push the upper body up into a push-up posture (however, with the legs flat on the floor and the toes pointed backward). Take a deep breath.

- Now move to the hands-and-knees position, as if you were going to crawl.

- Then curl your toes under so you can then push your rear end upward, forming an inverted V with arms being the front arm of the V and the rear end and legs the back arm of the V; keep your head pointed down and continue breathing. Walk your toes a few more inches forward so you can stretch out your calves and Achilles tendons.

- Now walk your right foot forward to get into a runner's starting position; as you do this, however, pull your head upward and drop your rear end downward so there is a gentle inverted arch in your back (or a sway).

- Move the right foot backward to the original position, and then walk the left foot forward, again in the runner's starting position, but again with your head raised upward and your rear end dropped toward the floor to put a sway in the back.

- Move the left foot back, stretch both Achilles tendons, and then lower yourself to the floor and roll over onto your back.

- Take about 5–7 minutes to merely rest now, lying completely flat and breathing deeply—belly out as you inhale, belly in as you exhale. You may also lie with back flat and knees bent upward and falling slightly together to take stress off the lumbar area of the spine. Just a suggestion: as you breath inward, say "Lord," and as you exhale, "have mercy." This keeps your intention and attention on the Lord, who is the One who heals you.

- At the end of the rest, slowly get back into the crossed-leg sitting position. You may close your time with the Lord's Prayer, a memorable song, or even a chant focused on a Scripture text.

You can download an illustrated version of this stretching and meditation workout routine at www.graceplacewellness.org. Then go to subheading, Programs, and then click on Christians in Movement and Meditation.

PAINTER/POINTER COMMUNICATION TYPOGRAPHY SCALE

REV. DR. DAVID LUDWIG

Circle the number that shows the degree to which one of the two descriptions fits your personality (3 is neutral).

1. When upset, can focus on something else and forget about things. 1 2 3 4 5 When upset, things stay stirred up inside and cannot easily be pushed aside.

2.* When upset, needs to be with others to talk over things. 5 4 3 2 1 When upset, needs space to be alone and let things settle down.

3.* Is comfortable feeling and expressing emotion 5 4 3 2 1 Feeling and expressing emotion is unsettling.

4. Is usually not tuned in to subtle emotional cues. 1 2 3 4 5 Is sensitive to subtle cues from others.

5. Can focus on one thing and be oblivious of other things going on. 1 2 3 4 5 When trying to concentrate on one thing, is also aware of other things going on.

6.* Can be doing many things at once—is good at shifting back and forth. 5 4 3 2 1 Is best at doing only one thing at a time—difficult to shift back and forth.

7. Tends to minimize the emotional importance of a situation (no big deal). 1 2 3 4 5 Tends to overstate the emotional importance for effect—to get through.

8. Will get right to the point; will summarize and give generalizations.	1 2 3 4 5	Will paint a picture—will give different details as they come to mind.
9.* Feels best when can be expressive and be the center of attention.	5 4 3 2 1	Is a good listener and feels best when the other person is in a good mood.
10. The first thing said is normally the point.	1 2 3 4 5	The first thing said is rarely the point.
11. When the other person is upset, will tend to withdraw.	1 2 3 4 5	When the other person is upset, will try to make contact.
12.* Will state feelings based on what is felt at the moment.	5 4 3 2 1	Will summarize feelings over time and state summary.
13.* Will tend to flash all possible scenarios so that will not be surprised.	5 4 3 2 1	Will tend to overlook what can go wrong so as to stay optimistic about things.
14.* Moods will fluctuate moment to moment.	5 4 3 2 1	Moods will usually stay fairly even.
15.* Will feel a definite emotional reaction; things seem black or white	5 4 3 2 1	Will tend to see different sides and be ambiguous as to how to react.

* indicated when the numbering is reversed, going in descending order from 5 to 1

Add the numbers up. If below 45, you have *pointer* tendencies. If above 45, you have *painter* tendencies.

Painter/Pointer Communication Typography Scale used with permission of Rev. Dr. David Ludwig.

BIBLE STUDY GUIDE FOR SMALL GROUPS

JOHN D. ECKRICH, M.D.

1. Water and the Word

Praying the Word of God (Word-Saturated Prayer) is a discipline with a strong Christian value and is part of many denominational traditions. Perhaps it is helpful to prepare a time of solitude and quiet as you approach God's Word. One begins by invitationally praying that the Holy Spirit is present in your time of prayer, and that the Spirit works God's Word and will within you as you reflect or meditate on the text. After meditation on the Word, an offering in prayer of your personal intentions and the aligning of your own will with God's can follow. Please see Diagram Four for one example of this type of prayer.

Texts for Reflection:

- Luke 2:19 Mary keeps all she has experienced and ponders them in her heart.
- Luke 10:38–42 Jesus visits Mary and Martha at Bethany.
- Matthew 6:5–14 Jesus teaches us the Lord's Prayer in the Sermon on the Mount.

Reflection Questions:

1. What prayer practices do you use in your daily communication with the Lord?

2. What prayer resources or guides do you find helpful in your prayer life?

3. Have you tried to meditate on the Word? If so, what has hindered your reflection time, and what has been beneficial to maintain focus during your time in the Word?

4. Do you use prayer lists, praying for different people or issues on each day?

5. Why would a time of quiet or solitude with Jesus be helpful as you enter a time of praying the Word?

Hymns and Songs:

- "O Holy Spirit, Enter In"
- "Come Holy Ghost, Our Souls Inspire"
- "Spirit of the Living God, Fall Afresh on Me"

Additions:

2. GPS—Family Support and Accountability

Maintaining good health habits and choices is difficult if we try to do so alone. Therefore our families—no matter what form that might take—can provide guidance, encouragement, and accountability. The family should be a place of *agape,* and a place where we learn communication, conflict management, and forgiveness. We realize that family patterns and interactions can be edifying or deflating.

Texts for Reflection:

Unhealthy family interactions:

- Genesis 25:19–34, 27:1–40 Rebekah favors Jacob over Esau and encourages deception.
- Genesis 37:18–36 Joseph is sold into slavery by his brothers.

Healthy family interactions:

- Genesis 42:1–38 Joseph forgives his brothers.
- Exodus 17:12 Aaron and Hur hold up Moses' arms.
- John 19:26–27 John takes Mary, Jesus' mother, into his home.
- Hebrews 10:24–25 Encouraging one another through our love.

Reflection Questions:

1. What makes up your family or support/accountability team? How might it be different from other families?

2. What does the term *agape* mean and how does it differ from other types of love?

3. What is healthy within the life of your family? If you are comfortable, what is not so healthy within your family interactions? (You may take personal quiet reflection of this question.)

4. How does your family help hold you accountable to healthy practices and choices?

Hymns and Songs:

- "Oh, Blest the House, Whate'er Befall"
- "Jesus Loves Me, This I Know"
- "For All the Saints Who from Their Labor Rest"
- "Blest Be the Tie that Binds"

Additions:

3. Granola Bar—Nutrition

We need healthy food and drink to smoothly run the gift of our bodies, minds, and emotions. Poor nutrition leading to obesity has become the number-one health issue in our land. When we make nutritional choices, we need to consider whether our short-term choices are consistent with our long-term health objectives. We remember we are caring for the "temple of the Holy Spirit."

Texts for Reflection:

- Genesis 1:1–19 God's good creation and the gift of fruit and vegetables.
- Genesis 9:3–4 God's gift of meat.
- Exodus 16:11–35 The gift of manna and the proper use of it.
- Matthew 14:13–21 The feeding of the 5,000.
- Matthew 26:17–30; Mark 14:12–26; Luke 22:7–39; John 13:1–17; 26 The Eucharist.
- 1 Corinthians 11:23–25 The new covenant in his blood.

Reflection Questions:

1. How many have ever tried to diet or eat more nutritionally? What has worked and what has not? Do you have insight as to why you have been either successful or unsuccessful in your nutritional strategies?

2. What type of support system do you have in place to help you with food choices?

3. What do you understand about the nutritional needs of those in your community both here in the U.S. as well as around the world?

4. What are you doing about hunger in the world within your family or within your community or faith community?

5. Do you still pray before or after meals? What are your family traditions surrounding food?

Hymns and Songs:

- "Feed Thy Children God Most Holy"
- "We Praise You, O God, Our Redeemer, Creator"
- "Give Thanks with a Grateful Heart"
- "For the Fruits of His Creation"
- "Lord of Glory, You Have Bought Us"

Additions:

4. Running Shoes—Exercise

All of God's creation is in motion. Our God is in motion. His Son was in motion throughout his earthly walk. God has created us to function best when we are able to be in motion properly and regularly. Exercise is good for our body (weight, bones, heart), and mind (moods and intellect, and dealing with stress).

Texts for Reflection:

- Numbers 20:11; Exodus 16:31 God moves (alters) creation for his people.
- Joshua 5:6 The children of Israel walk in the desert 40 years.
- Matthew 2:13 Joseph and Mary take flight to Egypt
- Matthew 3:13–17 God moves (sends) his Son and anoints him to save his people.
- Luke 24:13–32 The disciples on the road to Emmaus.

Reflection Questions:

1. What are adequate amounts of exercise time for good health of the heart? Of emotions?

2. What do you do in your own exercise disciplines that you find refreshing?

3. What time of day works best? Do you stretch, lift weights, and/or do aerobics?

4. What benefits do you experience from exercise?

5. Please share community resources for exercise that you are aware of for all.

Hymns and Songs:

- "Let Us Ever Walk with Jesus"
- "I Want to Walk as a Child of Light"
- "Onward Christian Soldiers"
- "We Walk by Faith and Not by Sight"
- "Greet the Rising Sun"

Additions:

5. Travel Pillow—Rest

Integral to God's creation is rest. He prioritizes it and it is a part of His Son's life and ministry. Rest might be divided into times of Sabbath (solitude and focus on our relationship with God) and leisure (non-work time, relaxation). Adequate and good quality of sleep is critical to the refreshing and resetting of body, mind, and spirit. God-pleasing leisure is renewing. There is a time for every purpose under heaven.

Texts for Reflection:

- Genesis 2:2–3 God rests after creation.
- Leviticus 25:2–7 Israel's guidelines for rest.
- Psalms 55:6; 127:2; 4:8 Invitation in the Psalms to rest.
- Matthew 1:20 Joseph is visited in dream by angel and receives clarity.
- Mark 6:31–32 Jesus rests.
- Matthew 8:23–27 Jesus sleeps in boat during a storm.
- Philippians 4:6–10; Hebrews 4:9–11 Rest for the children of God.

Reflection Questions:

1. Why do you think God builds into his creation the gift of rest?

2. Since all things are in motion, does rest require a lack of motion?

3. Do you keep times of Sabbath in you schedule? What does that look like in your life?

4. How do you balance work and rest?

5. We know that Satan works in times of work and times of rest to disrupt our relationship with God. What do you do to keep your times of *leisure* holy, or God-pleasing?

Hymns and Songs:

- "Be Still, My Soul"
- "Christ Be My Leader By Night and By Day"
- "Go, My Children, with My Blessing"
- "Great Is Thy Faithfulness"
- "Take My Life and Let It Be"
- "The Lord Is My Shepherd, I Shall Not Want"
- "You Who Dwell in the Shelter of the Lord"
- "Abide with Me, Fast Falls the Eventide"

Additions:

6. Two Pennies—Financial Stewardship and Generosity

We are stewards of all of God's creation. All is his and we are caretakers, but caretakers meant to be active in our service. The Lord cares primarily about your heart. Anxiety over our worldly possessions does not prosper us or our faith walk. A marker of good stewardship is our willingness to be generous.

Texts for Reflection:

- Luke 21:1–4 The widow's two coin offering.

- Mark 12:17 Appropriate sharing of our gifts.

- Matthew 25:20–21; Luke 12:42–46; Hebrews 13:5; Colossians 3:23; 1 Peter 4:10; Titus 1:7–9 Good stewardship of God's gifts.

- Matthew 6:5–34; Philippians 4:6–8 Do not be anxious over God's gifts.

- Luke 10:33–35 The Good Samaritan.

Reflection Questions:

1. What stewardship resources and principles do you use within your life and family? Please share these resources for others to be informed.

2. What causes you anxiety in your life?

3. Is stewardship purely a financial concern? Is there stewardship of other parts of your life that the Lord might be inviting you to care for?

4. For personal reflection, are you generous?

5. Do you demonstrate Good Samaritan activity within your faith community? If so, please elaborate. Where can your faith group do more?

Hymns and Songs:

- "Take My Life and Let It Be"
- "Lord of Glory, You Have Bought Us"
- "Give Thanks with a Grateful Heart"
- "We Praise You, O God, Our Redeemer, Creator"
- "The Gifts Christ Freely Gives"
- "The Common Doxology"

Additions:

7. Smartphones—Living and Serving in Community

God invites us to live and serve in community. It is not good to be alone all of the time. Face-time, whether on our smartphones or more effectively in person, is a far more valuable form of communication than texting. Our relationships are to be marked by curiosity about two books: the Scriptures and the books that are our family, friends, coworkers, and neighbors. Love and work as *we* rather than *me*. It is important to understand how people communicate (painters/pointers), to respect and honor their thoughts and communications, and to be forgiving, gentle, and patient in our relationships.

Texts for Reflection:

- Genesis 2:18 We are not to be alone on our earthly walk.

- Luke 8:40–48; John 4:4–42 Jesus is always curious about those he meets.

- John 4:7–9; Matthew 5:44 Jesus calls us to love and care for all, even our enemies and those we don't agree with or understand.

- Matthew 9:1–8 Jesus finds teaching moments in all interpersonal situations.

- John 13:34–35 Love one another.

- 1 John 4:20 Loving your brother.

- 1 Peter 4:8 Love one another and forgive.

- 1 Corinthians 13:1–13 What it means to love.

- Ephesians 4:1–32 Loving in the bond of peace—one Lord, one Faith, one Baptism.

Reflection Questions:

1. How does the concept of living and working as *we* rather than *me* affect your family life, vocation, and community?

2. Are you a painter or a pointer? (May want to refer to the painter/pointer test in appendix.) How does that affect your communication in these relationships?

3. Have you developed ways to honor others and their thoughts and feelings when you communicate with them?

4. Within conflicts in relationships, whose half of the relationship are you really able to manage; yours or the other person's?

5. Can you think of a person that you have a hard time forgiving? What is obstructing your forgiving? Is it possible for you, in the quiet place of your heart, to offer a prayer to have Jesus help you to forgive that person?

Hymns and Songs:

- "Let Us Ever Walk with Jesus"
- "Praise the One Who Breaks the Darkness"
- "Come Thou Fount of Every Blessing"
- "Where Charity and Love Prevail"
- "Jesu, Jesu, Fill Us with Your Love"
- "Love in Christ Is Strong and Living"
- "The Church's One Foundation"
- "Where Charity and Love Prevail"

Additions:

Wellness Backpack

FOR YOUR CHRISTIAN JOURNEY

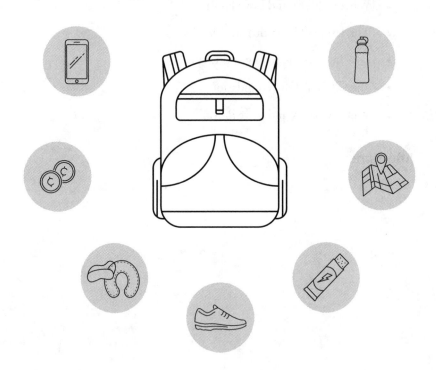